COLLECTING
TOY TRAINS

Pierce Carlson

COLLECTING
TOY TRAINS

Pierce Carlson

New Cavendish Books

London 1993

DEDICATION

This book is lovingly dedicated to my dear Eleanor. When we were young and years ago, the world was a cheerier and altogether hopeful place. Since then, among the darkening portents, Eleanor has remained as cheerful and hopeful as when I first met her in Boston, that far away New England capital. Time has changed us all. Hopes have faded and visions have dimmed but Eleanor, still brave and bright, provides the light for all of us who love her.

Author's note

Where included, the actual measurement of a gauge is given only in its original form - either in inches or in millimetres. No attempt has been made to give imperial or metric equivalents of gauge sizes. The table on page 154 lists all gauges used by the major manufacturers and indicates relative sizes.

Text © Pierce Carlson 1986
Collective work
© New Cavendish Books 1993

First published in hardback 1986
by Victor Gollancz Ltd
Paperback edition first published in 1993
by New Cavendish Books

British Library Cataloguing in Publication Data

Carlson, Pierce
  Toy Trains: a history.
  1. Railroads - Models - History
  I. Title
  745.592   TF197

New Cavendish Books Ltd.
3 Denbigh Road,
London W11 2SJ

ISBN 1 872727 56 5 (UK edition)
Printed and bound in Hong Kong
Produced by Manadarin Offset

Typeset by Keyspools Limited, Golbourne,
Ashdon, Lancashire

Published in the USA by
Pincushion Press
5245 Baywater Drive
Tampa, FL 33615

ISBN 1 883685 01 X (USA edition)

TITLE PAGES **Bing gauge IV set, 1900 (M); Marklin hanging lamp, 1904 (I)**

Gauge IV was the largest gauge (75mm) in the Bing catalogue. The Storkleg and 4-wheeled coaches, however, are very compact, and it is possible to construct a gauge IV railway that will fit into an average room or even on to a large table. The ability of the locomotive to take sharp curves, combined with the length of the coaches, which are shorter even than scale-length gauge OO coaches, means that interesting trains can be run over complex track layouts. The roofs of the coaches are hinged, and, with a little persuasion, a pet mouse or gerbil will be a reluctant passenger for a thrilling railway tour. The elegant plaster passengers are actually Japanese. *P. Carlson Collection*

OPPOSITE A 1902 steam-powered gauge III Single made by Carette in the livery of the Great Northern Railway.

CONTENTS

INTRODUCTION
THE MAGIC OF TOY TRAINS

One of the greatest inventions the world has ever known was that of the railway – nothing like it had ever been seen before, and the iron road opened up the world to vast numbers of people who had previously been rooted to their birthplace. All forms of travel had been slow, expensive and dangerous, but now, for the first time in history, the freedom to travel was available to everyone. Enterprising men everywhere quickly grasped the magnitude of the benefits that railways could offer and set to work; the scale of their endeavour was huge. In the 1890s, for example, Britain's London & North-Western Railway (L.N.W.R.) was the world's largest joint stock company; it designed and built its own locomotives and rolling stock, using steel supplied by its own steel plants.

Not only were the railways revolutionary in concept, but they were also built in a relatively short period of time. The network of tracks that rapidly spread over the land between 1830 and 1860 transformed people's lives to an undreamed-of extent, and, concomitantly, brought about great changes to the landscape. Railways had an enormous visual impact on town and country alike, and the change affected everyone.

For Americans, always a restless people, the railways meant more than just easier and faster travel. Railways were the key to the nation's survival as an entity. They allowed the vast new country to be united and governed, for not only could trains carry freight and passengers, they could also move and supply troops. It was, for instance, the mobility of the Northern armies that led to the defeat of the South and the preservation of the Union. In addition, the railways transported huge numbers of settlers on a great westward migration, which rapidly overwhelmed the thinly scattered Indians and Mexicans, and, almost overnight, the "Wild West" became "Smalltown, U.S.A." Without railways, a large and diverse country like the United States could not have survived for very long, and it is not surprising that early American locomotives were frequently decorated with flags, eagles and other patriotic emblems.

Trains, locomotives, carriages, tracks and stations entered into people's lives in an exciting new way. The poorest people, even if they could not afford a train trip, could at least visit a station. There is a theatrical quality about railway stations, where trains are both the actors and the drama itself. Certainly, the vast train sheds, second only to cathedrals in their immensity, were exciting enough, but the spectacle of the arrival of a crack express, all polished metal and clouds of steam, was a deeply thrilling sight. Whereas the workings of electricity or the telegraph were mysterious to many, the railways could be understood and appreciated by anybody.

Even small children knew how railways worked. They could walk alongside the train, touch the gleaming brass handles, hear the hiss of steam, the whistles and the clanking couplers and smell the hot oil. They could feel the heat coming from the boiler, say "hello" to the engine driver and give a frightened jump when the safety valve let off a powerful jet of steam.

People everywhere began to want to own something that represented a personal link with this awesome source of power, some bit of magic that could capture the soul of this great beast. Some people were content to record the numbers of the locomotives; others spent countless hours photographing every aspect of the railways; tickets were hoarded and tea was poured from locomotive-shaped teapots. But probably the most satisfying thing of all was to try to reduce the overpowering railway to the status of a pet, a miniature that would be under its owner's complete control. This impulse gave rise to toy railways.

Railway toys appeared almost simultaneously with the railways themselves, and children found that running a small train as they pleased was an intensely satisfying experience. It was, moreover, an experience that many were reluctant to give up once they were adults. Toy trains were quite often carefully packed away when their owners grew up, to remain undisturbed for decades, as pieces of powerful magic, and it is this magic that attracts the toy train collector. Somehow, the collector is able to recapture that fleeting childhood moment of power and control, and relive the moment when he was undisputed master of his own railway.

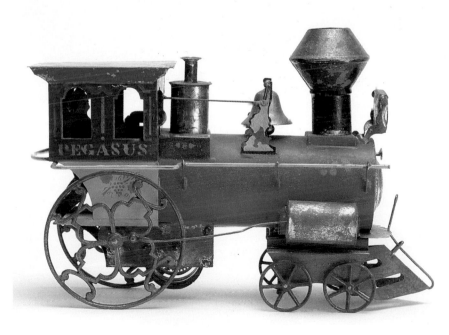

Stevens & Brown *Pegasus*, 1874 (M)
This large and impressive toy is representative of the type of toy train that was popular in the United States in the 1870s and 1880s. Although pure fantasy, the spirit behind the design conveys very well the impression of a wood-burning, brightly painted and high-stepping American steam locomotive of the period. The mechanism that causes the engineer to ring the bell is a wonderful feature that is seldom found in later toy trains.
D. Pressland Collection.

1
THE EVOLUTION OF THE TOY TRAIN 1840–90

The first toy trains were in the hands of children almost as soon as the first railways started running, for such an important step in the progress of civilization would not have gone unnoticed in the toy world. Some of the earliest toy trains were simple lead "flats", which the Germans made by pouring lead into engraved slate moulds, in the same way that flat lead soldiers were made. These trains were simple toys with a great deal of period charm but no moving parts, and they were intended to be included in miniature scenes together with flat figures, trees and buildings, all of which were made to the same approximate scale. The effect was charming but rather precious.

For more robust children who wanted toys with some action, woodcarvers in the German region of Erzegebirge made imaginatively crafted wooden trains with wheels that actually rolled. The methods used to produce the wooden trains were those used to produce the most popular toy made in Erzegebirge – the Noah's Ark – which was manufactured by a combination of simple machine tools and hand carving.

These lead and wooden toys were the popular and inexpensive mainstay of the German toy industry for the first half of the 19th century. Because of the ease with which lead and wooden toys could be produced, the German toy business was largely a cottage industry, controlled by a few large wholesale firms, which printed the catalogues and handled the distribution.

German tin toys of the same period tended to be elaborate constructions for the well-to-do. Germany was not yet an industrial power, and the German élite was a conservative class, which preferred toy horse-drawn carriages, dolls' houses and tin castles with real water

Lutz floor train, 1875 (J)
An exceptionally good example of a typical German floor train of the period before 1885; it is unusual to find one complete with wagons. *Christie's, London*

fountains. A few small family companies were producing the expensive tin toys, and Lutz, Rock & Graner, Mathias Hess, Gottfried Striebel and Buchner, were all well established firms by the mid-19th century. Little is known about these early German toy manufacturers, although Hess is known to have been established at Nuremberg by *c*.1826, when the company was making trackless, push-pull trains. These early makers were joined in 1859 by Theodore Märklin, who started to produce children's model cooking equipment and dolls' house furnishings at Göppingen, establishing there a mechanical and toy making business that was destined to become the most significant name in the world of toys, especially of toy trains.

Many German toy manufacturers established factories in Nuremberg during the second half of the 19th century, for the tin mines were close and there was plenty of cheap, but skilled, labour. The Frenchman Georges Carette migrated to Nuremberg in 1896, attracted not only by the work already being produced there but also by the comparatively low German wages and the skilled toy and clock makers. By the 1890s, Nuremberg was poised to become the mecca of European toy train production.

SCIENTIFIC TOYS FROM BRITAIN AND FRANCE
Britain, the birthplace of the railway, and the nation that led the Industrial Revolution, took an appropriately serious view of the toy locomotive, and early British products were usually proper locomotives, propelled by steam and made from solid brass. Ironically, these technically advanced and relatively expensive toys, which were made from the mid-1840s, are known today as "dribblers" or, worse, "piddlers," from the trail of water deposited by their steam cylinders. "Dribblers" came in countless different sizes and gauges and, like most of the toy locomotives, appeared to be patterned after the very earliest prototype trains, such as the 2-2-2 "Planets" or 0-4-0 "Burys".* "Dribblers" were almost always made without cabs, usually having no more than a spectacle plate, and they generally had wonderful names like *Thunderer*, *Britannia*, *Invicta*, *Empress Queen* and *Zulu*.

These early designs seem to have been produced for decades without change. Stevens's Model Dockyard, of 22 Aldgate, London, perhaps the best known firm to produce "dribblers", and whose history went back to 1843, manufactured at least 18 different designs and still had "dribblers" in its catalogue in 1926.

Although these locomotives look quaint and crude by today's standards, they were considered technological marvels in the 19th century. Manufacturers such as H. J. Wood, a London-based instrument maker and professional model builder, and Newton & Co. of 3 Fleet

Stevens's Model Dockyard "dribbler" of 1900. This steamer was made in a wide, but non-standard, gauge.

---

*Locomotives are described according to the "Whyte" system of classification: the first figure indicates the number of leading wheels, the second figure the number of driving wheels and the third figure the number of trailing wheels.

Street, Temple Bar, London, a respected firm of scientific instrument makers, made outstandingly accurate models. In fact, the finish used for telescopes and scientific apparatus – usually polished brass with decorative bands of oxidized brass – was a typical finish for British brass locomotives. It had nothing to do with any prototype livery.

The wheels on the "dribblers" were usually a discreet dark green, never vulgar red, and the coaches and wagons were made of polished mahogany. This finish is a clue to the British attitude toward toy trains during the heyday of these early locomotives. "Dribblers" were regarded as scientific toys, which would teach the mysteries of the Victorian prime mover, the steam locomotive, to the interested purchaser; they were not merely toys that children would have fun playing with.

Several firms competed with one another in the production of "dribblers", and each firm developed its own range of locomotives, from the small and cheap to the large and expensive. It is difficult not only to identify British manufacturers but also to determine exactly which companies produced what, for the exchange of design details, fittings and

even complete locomotives seems to have been common. However, in addition to Stevens's Model Dockyard and Newton & Co. of London, it is known that "dribblers" were produced by, among others, John Theobald, London; Lucas & Davies, London; Clyde Model Dockyard, Glasgow (established in 1789); Whitney's of London; British Modelling & Electric Co., Leek, Staffordshire (established 1884); J. Bateman & Co., London (established in 1774); Jones & Co.; and H. Wiles, Manchester.

Many firms produced extensive catalogues in which they claimed that they were manufacturing all the products advertised, when, in reality, they were not manufacturing anything themselves. Many manufacturers padded out their own ranges with the products of other British companies and even foreign firms. An 1870s catalogue from Clyde Model Dockyard included products from the French firm of Radiguet and from the German firms of Plank, Bing and Schönner, as well as its own. However, firms were loathe to admit that the items they advertised were not made entirely by themselves, and it is interesting to quote from the Introduction to the 1926 (and last) Stevens's Model Dockyard catalogue:

Stevens's Model Dockyard was established in 1843, for the purpose of encouraging the rising generation, amateur mechanics, &c., in scientific research, mechanical recreations and instructive amusements. Since then, owing to the success of Stevens's Model Dockyard other imitations calling themselves "Model Dockyards" have started all over the country, principally of the common toy-shop and bazaar class, who do not manufacture any of their goods, but sell inferior English or foreign-made ships, engines, fittings, &c., which are made of such flimsy, and trumpery materials that they are quite useless for practical purposes and fail to give satisfaction to their purchasers. Our establishment is entirely devoted to mechanical and scientific amusements, and we do not deal or sell in any way children's ordinary toys such as Noah's Arks, rocking horses, fancy goods, &c. The present proprietors are practical mechanics, having served their apprenticeship, and have been in this business all their lives, and have practical knowledge of all kinds of model steam engines, ships, boats and the fittings appertaining to them. All the ships, boats, engines, boilers, parts and fittings are made under their personal supervision in our own workshops by an efficient plant of up-to-date tools and staff of skilled workmen. The public are warned not to be deceived by fancy engravings and untrue statements in catalogues that are published of model engines, ships, fittings, &c. We guarantee that we are genuine manufacturers of our own models, parts and fittings, and that the engravings in this catalogue are taken from the original articles, so that all purchasers can see what they are buying. We have been compelled to make this statement owing to the dishonest piracy of our catalogue, advertisements, patterns, &c., by unscrupulous traders ...

German flat lead train set, 1860 (C); German flat lead castles, 1880 (A); German Erzegebirge wooden train set, 1870 (C); Ortelli (Spanish) flat lead train set, 1880 (B); semi-flat lead railway figures, 1905 (A)
The first toy trains made in Germany were small toys of lead and wood, which could easily be made by a toy industry that was still "cottage" based. The trains were usually a by-product of the toy soldier trade, and they were made in the same manner: by casting a lead/tin mixture into slate moulds. Since many of these moulds have survived, it is very difficult to distinguish between recent production and early examples. The Erzegebirge trains come from ancient German traditions of wood carving, and they were sold over long periods with little change to the designs. The Spanish train is a rare example from the long, vigorous tradition of Spanish toy making. Although inspired by similar early German trains, the design retains a uniquely Spanish flavour. *Courtesy London Toy and Model Museum; P. Carlson Collection*

After this fiery blast, it is worth noting that one page alone of the catalogue contains no fewer than four illustrations of locomotives from the Nuremberg firm of Carette, their trademarks carefully removed.

Apart from the army of "dribblers", very few British toy trains of the 19th century have survived. William Britain & Son, better known for its toy soldiers, made a little lead train in the 1860s; it was pulled around in a circle by an external clockwork motor. One or two examples of clockwork floor-runners made of tin have also survived, as have a small number of cast-iron trains made c.1892 by Wallwork, a Manchester-based iron foundry. Wallwork appears to have been the only British manufacturer to have used cast iron to make toy trains. The company's catalogue listed only two styles of locomotives and some coaches, which looked as if they were modelled on trains in use during the 1840s. The spacing of the wheels was quite wide, which gave a feeling of the G.W.R. broad gauge, and some of the locomotives were finished with coupling rods. None of Wallwork's cast-iron trains appears to have had any mechanisms.

In France at least one firm, Radiguet & Massiot, went along with the British in producing brass "dribblers". Radiguet founded a company in Paris in 1872, which primarily made scientific and educational instruments. In 1889 he went into partnership with Massiot, and the company produced many parts for British toy train firms, which claimed to be manufacturers. Some British companies even sold Radiguet toy trains as their own, and in fact it takes an expert to distinguish a Radiguet from its British cousin. However, the larger Radiguet "dribblers" have a certain elegance that is unmistakably French. Examples of Radiguet locomotives appear in almost every British toy train catalogue of the 1880s and 1890s,

Hall's patent British floor train, 1885 (G) British tin floor trains from this period are almost non-existent. The design of this one is not particularly British in outline, but the working whistle adds charm. *Phillips*

which is rather surprising in view of the multitude of British "dribblers" on offer. However, they might have been advantageously priced. Radiguet produced a vast range of rather archaic designs, but the company's success did not seem to inspire any other French competitors, for Radiguet remained the sole significant manufacturer of model steam locomotives in France until the end of the century.

Radiguet, however, was far from being the only toy train manufacturer in France. Countless small firms were marketing toy trains in considerable numbers as early as 1835. The French, being master tinsmiths, turned to thin sheet tin for the majority of their toy trains. They were simply constructed, and the tin was usually embossed to give it some added strength. The trains had no rails but ran happily on the floor, occasionally helped by clockwork but, more often, just pushed or pulled by hand. The paintwork was delightful but did not adhere well to the tin, and today it is rare to find an early French floor train with the paintwork intact. Cheaper versions were spirit-painted, which gave a translucent finish and lasted moderately well, but the colours were liable to fade, especially when left in direct sunlight.

All the early French trains have tremendous charm, and the larger specimens are true fantasies of marvellous delicacy, rolling on spidery spoked wheels and sporting tall, ornate chimneys. The clockwork-powered examples had the usual, finely made French motors, which were

ABOVE French floor train, 1865 (D)
Very small, early French floor trains are not too difficult to find in poor condition; this one, however, has unusually good paint. There is no mechanism and the modelling is minimal, yet this little train still manages to capture the spirit of the first railways. *Sotheby's, London*

BELOW F.V. French floor train, 1865 (H)
F.V. (Emile Favre), a pioneering French manufacturer, made this fine floor train, which has simulated wooden boiler lagging and lettering on painted, stuck-on labels. Floor trains of this size usually had quite powerful clockwork mechanisms *Sotheby's, London*

very strong for their size. The French were interested in complete trains, and their toy locomotives were quite often followed by tin coaches and wagons, usually rolling on frail lead wheels.

Toy trains were popular in France, and during the 1880s they were probably more widespread than in either Britain or Germany. There were several manufacturers, most of which were known simply by their initials: F.V. (Emile Favre et E.F. LeFèvre Successeurs), C.R. (Charles Rossignol), D.S. (Dessin), J.C. (J. Caron), G.P. (Georges Parent, successor to Maltête & Parent) and L.G. (Paris). Of these the most important were Rossignol and Favre.

Charles Rossignol founded the company that bore his name in Paris in 1868. At first the firm produced floor trains, later turning to tin-plate cars and buses. Rossignol's great skill in lithography transformed his rather basic floor-runners into masterpieces of toy art. The company made no attempt to make locomotives to scale, but a fantastic array of

COLLECTING

TOY TRAINS

Pierce Carlson

PRICE GUIDE

The caption for each train illustrated in this book includes a letter (from A to M) indicating the price range of that particular item. Auction prices can, of course, vary widely, but the price range given here is a realistic indication of the value of each item.

A	less than £25	less than $40
B	£20-£60	$30-$90
C	£45-£100	$70-$150
D	£75-150	$120-$225
E	£100-£200	$150-$300
F	£150-£300	$225-$450
G	£250-£500	$375-$750
H	£400-£850	$600-$1275
I	£750-£1250	$1150-$1900
J	£1000-£1500	$1500-$2300
K	£1250-£2000	$1900-$3000
L	£1500-£2500	$2250-3750
M	more than £2000	more than $3000

Newton 2-2-2, 1890 (l)
One of the attractive features of this well-made product of a British instrument maker is the handsomely engraved plate on the boiler giving the manufacturer's name and address. Although these locomotives were equipped with flanged wheels, they were intended to run on the floor. Most examples of this type of early locomotive were supplied without tenders, and it is quite unusual for this Newton "dribbler" to have a tender.
P. Carlson Collection

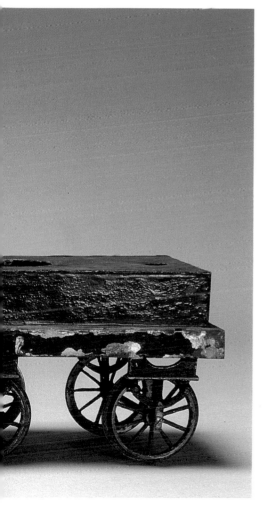

gadgets was lithographed on to otherwise unadorned superstructures, coaches had window shades at different heights, and even a dust and grime effect was lithographed on the lower portion of the body.

Emile Favre et E.F. LeFèvre Successeurs (F.V.) was founded in 1860 and specialized in the manufacture of mechanical tin-plate toys. It was probably the earliest company anywhere to provide a range of accessories to complement its trains. The pastel-painted tin stations were very evocative of French railway scenes and were set off nicely by the signals, signs, sheds and occasional tin tree. However, rails were not made for these early French railways, and without rails and switch points, toy railroading was not possible. When it was provided, F.V. track was nothing more than a circle of tin with a couple of grooves pressed into it, and there was no possibility for expansion beyond the circle shape. Toy railroads required standardization and precision, qualities that French toy manufacturers did not regard highly. They much preferred artistic flair, decorative design and charm – but it is precisely these qualities that are prized by today's toy train collector.

In general, the toy world in Britain and Europe was rather retrospective in design. All the mid-19th century toy manufacturers seemed reluctant to model anything that was in any way up-to-date or contemporary. Even quite late in the 1880s and early 1890s, French and British toy locomotives were based on prototypes that had been running forty or fifty years previously and "Planet" 2-2-2s, Stephenson Long Boilered 0-6-0s, "Burys" and Norris-types abounded. Very few had cabs, and many had simulated wood lagging on the boilers, a feature that had long disappeared on the real locomotives.

MASS PRODUCTION IN THE UNITED STATES
In the United States toy trains were very different from those in Europe. The thinly spread, relatively small population of the United States was separated by vast geographic distances, and as early as the 1830s manufacturers were beginning to be aware of the demand for miniature replicas of the exciting and impressive trains that were beginning to link up the country. However, for a company to succeed, it had to advertise, to be prepared to ship goods long distances and to mass produce. Factories had to be built and mass-production methods developed in order to sell at competitive prices. The methods of the European artisan workshops were not applicable to these conditions, and American toys tended to be simpler, larger and more rugged than their European counterparts. The American toy train had to be stronger than the exquisite and delicate French trains, larger and more sophisticated than the German lead and wood trains and cheaper than the British brass "dribblers".

The United States saw the development of the archetypal toy train: a distinctive design, made from a few basic, simple shapes and constructed from relatively heavy tin plate. In this design, all the basic features of an American locomotive existed in a cheerfully exaggerated form. The most popular types had two large driving wheels under the cab and two smaller wheels under the chimney. The wheels were very decorative and thin, but made from strong cast iron, which in many cases incorporated delightful and exuberant arabesques of hearts or geometric designs. Bells, lamps and cowcatchers complemented the large cabs and tall smokestacks.

Some expensive locomotives had working whistles and even smoked – if you put a cigarette down the chimney first. Cheaper versions were simple push-pull toys, while heavy, clockwork-powered locomotives were the top of the range. They were always finished in gaily coloured enamel, with lots of bright red and gold. Cabs and boilers were decorated with elaborate and bizarre patterns of flowers, dots, hearts, tiny triangles and other feathery flourishes, usually applied with stencils, to liven up what would otherwise be a rather plain basic design. The decoration had nothing at all to do with any prototype but was merely an inexpensive way of giving the toy more character.

Unlike France, where complete trains were popular, in the United States the toy was considered to be just the locomotive, with a tender and the rest of the train only occasionally included. Coaches and wagons are much rarer than locomotives. Rails were unheard of, as were accessories, and the imaginative child made stations from shoe boxes and tunnels from piled up books. There were no live steamers in mid-19th-century American nurseries: they were too expensive to manufacture and were considered dangerous for young children to use. The idea that adults might like to play trains had not yet occurred to Americans.

Between 1860 and 1890, the heyday of the American tin train, the major manufacturers were Ives, established in Plymouth, Connecticut, in 1868; Althof Bergmann & Co. of New York; Hull & Stafford of Clinton, Connecticut; Francis, Field & Francis, of Philadelphia, whose foreman, James Fallows, started his own factory in the same city; and Union Manufacturing Co.

According to tradition, the very first American manufacturer to produce clockwork trains was George W. Brown & Co., of Forestville, Connecticut, the centre of the clock making industry in the United States. The tin-plate clockwork trains first appeared in 1856, and by the 1860s production of similar models was in full swing across the country.

It is remarkable that, during the three decades (1860–90) when the American tin train enjoyed its greatest popularity, none of the manufacturers ever developed their basic designs, and locomotives produced in the 1890s looked exactly like those produced 30 years earlier.

When development did take place, it was in two entirely different – and peculiarly American – manufacturing materials: paper-covered wood and cast iron. Because of the expense of American labour compared with European labour at that time, American manufacturers were always on the look-out for ways to reduce the labour element of their costs.

Glueing lithographed paper on to simple wooden or cardboard

shapes was a cheap way of finishing a simple toy in order to make it look exciting. The large and brightly coloured toys made in this way were cheap and popular, although their survival rate was not high, and good examples today are hard to find and highly prized by collectors. The two major manufacturers were R. Bliss of Rhode Island and Milton Bradley of Springfield, Massachusetts; the latter is still in business today.

Casting iron had several advantages. Skilled labour costs could be confined to mould making and foundry operation, while assembly and finishing, which were greatly simplified, could be given to unskilled workers. Complex detail could be incorporated in the mould without adding greatly to the cost of the finished product. The result was a very different-looking toy train. The proportions of the cast-iron locomotive became more realistic because the iron castings were stronger and less susceptible to damage when they were long and narrow. Assembly was simple and usually consisted of a right-hand and a left-hand body casting to which wheels were added. Because of the greatly increased detail in moulding, the painting could be quite simple – often done by dipping – in one colour, usually black or red, but the toy would still look interesting. Lettering, if any, was applied by rubber stamp. The new cast-iron trains

Milton Bradley wooden floor train, 1885 (G)

Because American toys were almost entirely made in factories, there was always a keen interest in cutting labour costs. By glueing lithographed paper on to simple wood shapes, quite a pleasing toy could be produced. Firms such as Milton Bradley have made toys in this way for over a hundred years, but the method was never very popular in Europe, and virtually all examples of this type of toy are American. The superb period lithography adds considerable interest to what would otherwise be rather boring, flat surfaces. *Courtesy London Toy and Model Museum*

were usually sold complete with tenders and frequently passenger or freight cars were added to make a complete toy train.

The first of the established American companies to manufacture cast-iron trains was Ives, which was making trackless, push-pull and clockwork locomotives and trains in cast iron by the 1880s, listing them in its catalogues alongside its antiquated tin locomotives.

Ives was quickly joined by other firms: Kenton Hardware Co., of Kenton, Ohio; Arcade of Freeport, Illinois; Dent of Fullerton, Pennsylvania; Francis Carpenter of New York; Hubley of Lancaster, Pennsylvania; and Pratt & Letchworth of New York. J. & E. Stevens of Cromwell, Connecticut, and Wilkins of Medford, Massachusetts, were among the more prominent manufacturers. Cast iron is an extremely heavy material, and only a very few of the new cast-iron locomotives were powered by clockwork motors, while those that had motors did not pull trains. The largest cast-iron trains made by Pratt & Letchworth and Wilkins achieved standards of realism in outline that were not equalled until the 1930s. However, no matter how realistic cast-iron trains looked, they remained merely floor trains, which had to be pushed by hand. There were no rails or other accessories, although the enterprising young railroader could use a few well-detailed cast-iron still banks for stations and town buildings.

American floor train, 1880 (H)
Wooden trains like this one, possibly by Bliss, were usually decorated with lithographed paper stuck on to the sides. The train shown here, with an assortment of other toys made in the same way, provides a graphic demonstration of the considerable charm and appeal of period lithography. The roofs can be removed so that other toys, such as the blocks, may be stored inside. *Sotheby's, New York*

Introduced in the 1880s, cast-iron trains remained in production until the 1930s. Like the American tin trains, the designs were seldom updated, so that by 1930 the cast-iron trains of the 1880s and 1890s looked quite old fashioned. No other country with a toy industry ever used cast iron to the same extent as the United States. Casting iron was primarily a factory technique suitable for mass production, and it was beyond the capacity of the European cottage industries and artisan workshops. Only one manufacturer outside the United States seemed to be interested in cast iron, and that was the British firm of Wallwork (see page 12).

In a nation heavily engaged in building the world's greatest steam railway network there must have been a growing interest in a toy locomotive that was more advanced than the cast-iron nursery floor-runners. In 1872, Eugene Beggs of Patterson, New Jersey, started marketing a well-designed toy steam locomotive. It was a very smart locomotive, modelled on the popular 4-4-0 American types of the period, although the wheel arrangements included 2-2-2s and 4-2-0s as well as 4-4-0s.

Beggs provided strip rails so that the locomotive could travel in a circle. The axles were set at a radius, so that if the locomotive was running without the rails and directly on the floor, it would still travel in a circle. To complement the locomotive, lightweight coaches and sleeping cars with beautifully printed paper sides were made. The decoration of the locomotive contrasted with the realism of the coaches and consisted of splashes of paint applied artistically to the super-structure, similar to the finish of the tin floor-runners. The paint was set off by nickel-plated fittings and a cut glass headlamp.

For nearly thirty years, until the end of the century, the steam sets made by Beggs, and later by Garlick, once associated with Beggs, represented the best available American toy trains. However, the Beggs sets were expensive, and not everyone could afford the $10.00 to $30.00 price tag at a time when a dollar a day was considered a good wage. In 1888, to fill the gap at the lower end of the market, the enterprising Weeden Company introduced a lovely little steam locomotive called the *Dart*. It was an 0-4-0 of beautiful proportions, with rivet detail and a pair of dummy pilot wheels stamped from tin. A very light-gauge tin coach and tender completed the train, and it was sold with a circle of track for

Wilkin's floor train, 1885 (H)
American cast-iron floor trains were, in general, more realistic than the toy trains designed to run on tracks, and the large Wilkins captures perfectly the angular proportions of an American 4-4-0 of the 1880s. Four-wheeled cabooses were popular with the manufacturers of cast-iron trains, and examples such as these probably influenced Märklin's decision to produce a similar caboose in tin plate especially for the American market.
Sotheby's, New York

American cast-iron floor train, 1895 (G); French tin-plate floor train, 1880 (l)
There were considerable differences in the approaches taken to toy train manufacture by French and American firms in the later part of the 19th century. The Americans like cast iron, the plastic of the day, because it was suitable for the mass production of strong toys, able to stand up to a lot of abuse, and the assembly and finishing could be done by unskilled labour. The American toys were made in large numbers for a mass market and tended to reflect contemporary progress, such as the "Limited Vestibule Express" shown here. The French trains, on the other hand, were lightweight and were laboriously made in small numbers by skilled tinsmiths. The small and wealthy French élite, who bought the more elaborate trains, preferred toys that reflected some degree of historical remove, and the dawn of train travel, when passengers travelled in what looked like stage coaches, was a favourite period. *Courtesy London Toy and Model Museum*

between $3.00 and $3.75. It was instantly popular, and tens of thousands were sold. Several American manufacturers later used the same 2in gauge as Weeden.

Even to modern eyes, accustomed to reviewing the latest in scale models, the rivet detail, general delicacy and refinement of proportion of the *Dart* have great appeal and make later efforts by more famous firms look clumsy by comparison. The untimely death of William Weeden in 1889 halted any further development of the engine, although a larger, but less popular, version was brought out by his company, then under the direction of William Ritschie, about ten years later.

INDUSTRIALIZATION IN GERMANY

In Germany, meanwhile, following the lead set by Britain and France, industrialization was rapidly taking place. The new industrial confidence was matched by new political energy, fuelled by the successful war with France (1870), which was followed in 1871 by the realization of the dreams of 1848 – the unification of Germany. Toy firms sprang up to supply all kinds of modern and up-to-date toys that would help to sweep away the old image of a backward and rural Germany, dependent on cottage industry. The new and affluent middle class wanted toys that would reflect their new interests: steam trains, factories, steamships, soldiers, fire engines and all manner of scientific developments.

Between 1850 and 1900 over a dozen great toy making firms started up: Karl Bub in 1851, Märklin in 1859, Issmayer in 1861, Bing in 1865, Plank in 1866, Schönner in 1875, Günthermann in 1877, Lehmann in 1881, Carette in 1886, Fleischmann in 1887, Falk and Doll in 1898 and Distler in 1899. With the exceptions of Märklin (which was located at

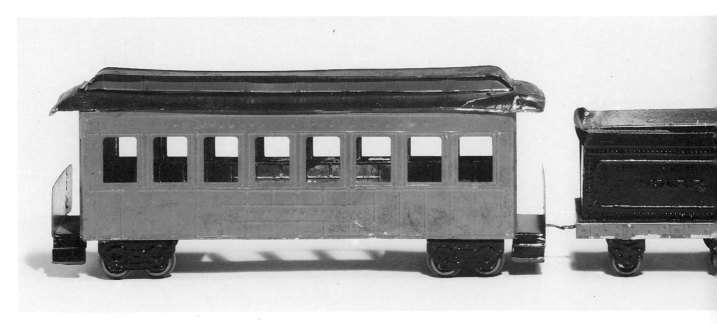

Göppingen) and Lehmann (which was based in Brandenburg), all these companies were founded in Nuremberg, which quickly became the toy centre of Europe. In no other country at the time was there such a group of ambitious, talented and well-financed firms preparing to take the world toy markets by storm. The motto of the Günthermann firm was *Die Ganze welt – ist mein Feld!*, that is, "The whole world is my field!"

Obviously the German domestic market was not large enough to absorb the output of so many firms – each one produced numerous different lines and a bulging annual catalogue – so the German firms began to look to Britain, France and the United States for both inspiration and new markets. Plank and Schönner copied the British "dribbler" designs, improved them and exported them back to Britain. Günthermann manufactured and then exported American-style 4-4-0s with cowcatchers to the United States. Schönner produced an astonishing range of steam-powered floor-runners for the United States, which were totally different from the designs exported to Britain. The small, French, tin-plate floor trains were studied and improved upon by Hess, Issmayer and Bing.

Several firms, notably Issmayer, Hess and Lehmann, had been working on lithographic printing, cheap clockwork mechanisms and new methods for assembling tin-plate toys by means of tabs and slots rather than by soldering. The use of lithography meant that toys no longer had to be laboriously hand painted; instead they could have a printed finish that was cheaper but that, if care was taken with the printing and graphics, could actually look far superior to hand-painted toys. Many of the companies – notably Bing, Carette and Günthermann – started to use lithography as soon as they could, but Märklin continued

Weeden *Dart*, 1888 (H)
This famous American steam locomotive was an enormous success in its day, and thousands were sold. It boasted such refinements as rivets on the boiler, an embossed name-plate and realistic, thin-spoked drivers. In comparison, the contemporary German efforts looked very crude. The coach was made from very thin tin, as light as possible, so that the performance of the little locomotive would remain lively. The photograph shows that the steam cylinder has become disconnected and is pointing straight up. *Sotheby's, New York*

to enamel most of its locomotives and rolling stock and used lithography only reluctantly for a limited range of cheap items.

American factory and mass-production methods had impressed the German manufacturers, and the best features of American organization were incorporated into the new German factories. Small Issmayer trains were exported in quantity to the United States, and the company had a range of lithographed locomotives and coaches that was distinctly American in outline and was grandly titled *Pacific Express Line*, an indication of Issmayer's plans to sweep across the United States from New York to San Francisco.

In the 1880s Issmayer developed a design for sectional tin-plate track, which used hollow, rolled-tin rails, fastened to tin ties and joined by pins fitted into the rails. Quite large railways could be constructed from just two types of short rail sections, curved and straight. Issmayer itself seemed to have failed to realize the significance of its sectional track system, and its small train sets – Issmayer's most popular small gauge was slightly narrower than gauge O – usually contained just enough curved track to make a small circle.

All the best features of the clever French mechanisms were carefully studied by the German manufacturers, modified for cheap mass production and incorporated into the rapidly growing German toy technology. The very lightweight clockwork motors, which used stamped gears and wire springs, were most suitable for the very small floor trains, and Lehmann, in particular, ingeniously reduced mechanisms down to their simplest and cheapest forms while still ensuring a reasonable degree of reliability.

In the 1880s, steam was the motive power preferred by the Germans to move anything with a bit of weight to it. The most common application of steam was the stationary steam engine, or steam plant, of which countless different designs in several different sizes were available. The early steam engine specialists were Schönner and Plank, and they quickly assimilated British steam technology and applied it to improved steam locomotive designs. Schönner and Plank were soon joined by Bing, Carette, Doll and Märklin. It is thought that some early Carette and Bing locomotives might have actually been manufactured by Schönner. This type of co-operation – inter-company sales and sub-contracting – was common practice at this time in the German toy industry, and every company gained from the arrangement for it meant that each company could offer a large catalogue of toys of every design, spread over a wide price range.

The decades before 1896 were not ones of prominence for the firm of Märklin. Products made by Märklin before 1890 are difficult to identify and appear to be largely concerned with toy kitchen equipment, furniture and accessories for dolls' houses and a modest line of horse-drawn vehicles. Elaborate miniature kitchen cooking ranges, complete with pots and pans, were the pride of the line.

This domestic bias reflected the personal interests of Frau Märklin,

Queen Victoria's royal train, German manufacture, 1875 (M)
Among the rarest of all toys is this magnificent train made specifically for the British royal family. Loosely modelled on the first royal saloon and train of the early 1840s, the manufacturer appears to be the German firm of Lutz, with, perhaps, the assistance of one of the early German locomotive makers such as Plank or Schönner. Intended for Prince Albert Victor, then heir to the throne, and Prince George (later King George V), it was given away to a member of the royal household after Prince Albert Victor's untimely death in 1892. Although designed as a floor-runner, the axles are not radial, so that the train can run only in a straight line. The coaches are completely equipped with glass windows, and they have elaborate interiors with mirrors and imitation marble tables. *P. Carlson Collection*

who had run the business single-handed since the death in 1866 of her husband, Theodor, the firm's founder. In 1888, two sons, Eugen and Karl, took control of the company, which then became known as Gebrüder Märklin, the name under which it traded until 1892. The Märklin brothers were young, still in their twenties, energetic and ambitious. Although the firm had been doing well with the pots and pans, the time had come for change, and things looked promising for Gebrüder Märklin.

At the same time, the long-established North German firm of Lutz was experiencing difficulties. The toys made by Lutz were top quality, expensive but beautifully made, and they had a superb finish. They were also innovative and technically advanced. Lutz made beautiful boats, elaborate fortresses, horses and carriages that were driven by clockwork, clockwork roundabouts, fire engines and water pumps, as well as toys driven by steam engines. However, from Märklin's point of view, the most significant toys made by Lutz were clockwork locomotives that ran on rails, for which sectional track was supplied.

Lutz toys were not, however, the kind that could be produced quickly or cheaply, and Lutz was being forced out of its traditional market. Märklin, on the other hand, had experience of volume production and an extensive distribution network. The two firms were complementary, and when Märklin incorporated Lutz in 1891, it did more than add Lutz toys to its catalogue: it absorbed the Lutz technology, expertise and product development, and it was able to capitalize on the excellent reputation that Lutz had acquired. In effect, Märklin became a new company in 1891, and, under its young directors, it was to prove in future decades to be the most dynamic and successful of all the vigorous new German toy companies.

A Carette gauge I steamer, dating from 1897.

2
THE INVENTION OF THE TOY RAILWAY SYSTEM 1890–1900

Until 1891 most manufacturers and buyers still tended to think of toy trains as they would toy boats, roundabouts or tops – they thought of the toys as objects that were complete in themselves. Railways, however, are different; they are not just objects, they are systems, and the locomotive, although dramatic and appealing, is just part of a larger, overall system.

Some manufacturers had, during the 1880s, become gradually aware that the locomotive toy alone was not enough. They had been adding tenders, passenger coaches, the passengers themselves, wagons, stations, and even, as an afterthought, rails for the toy train to run upon. In 1887, for example, Schönner supplied straight rails (but no curved ones) for its large and impressive American-styled steam locomotives, which had locked wheels so that only travel in a straight line was possible. On the other hand, the firm's "dribblers" were supplied with only circular track – quite logically, since, with all its axles set at a radius, it was impossible for the train to go in a straight line. But the idea of a figure-of-eight track plan was beyond the comprehension of most toy train manufacturers.

Things were soon to change, however, and a revolution in the world of toy trains was about to occur. The annual Leipzig Toy Fair was the major trade fair, and manufacturers showed their new products there and promoted lines to their international customers. For the 1891 Fair Märklin produced a series of new train sets that proved to be milestones in the history of the toy train.

Having incorporated the Lutz toy trains into its own lines and simplified them so that they could be produced in a reasonable volume and at a reasonable price, Märklin had made for the Leipzig Toy Fair a range of toy trains in three different sizes. The sizes were designated I, II and III, and each one called for a different track gauge – that is to say, a different distance between the rails. The smallest size was gauge I, at 48mm ($1\frac{3}{4}$in) between the rails; gauge II was 54mm (2in) and the largest, at 75mm (3in), was gauge III.

Not only did Märklin exhibit the gauge system, which was to prove of immense significance in the toy train world, but the company also invented and demonstrated at the Fair two brand new pieces of track: the switch point and the cross-over, which allowed a figure-of-eight track plan. The crossing was at an angle of 53° and the figure-of-eight geometry was not quite correct, but, no matter, the connecting pins could be bent a little, and the kinks in the track gave a little realism to the whole operation. To complement the revolutionary concept, the skilled Lutz tinsmiths also created a station and a few accessories.

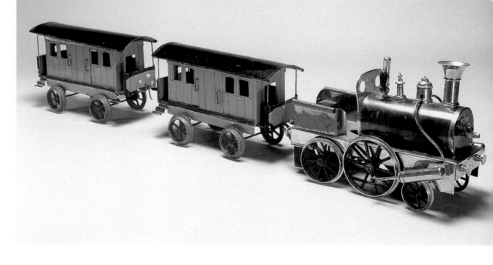

ABOVE Märklin/Lutz 75mm gauge train, 1894 (M)

This is a train from the dawn of the German toy train era and one that illustrates the early German approach to toy trains. Although extremely large, it is still a practical toy for children, and it will run around a fairly small circle of track. Everything is well made and beautifully hand painted, but still relatively simple. Details are few but bold, and the whole train has a wonderful old railway feel to it. Whether it is by Lutz or Märklin is a moot point, since Lutz was absorbed into the Märklin organization at about the time this train was manufactured.

Courtesy London Toy and Model Museum

LEFT Schönner gauge III set, 1894 (J)
Illustrated here is one of the first train sets by Schönner that was designed to run on tin rails. The rails had to be in a circle because the radial axle settings of the locomotive and coaches meant that only right-hand bends could be negotiated. Schönner's locomotive design at this period shows considerable British influence, and this example could be mistaken for a British "dribbler". Most sets were supplied with a coach and a baggage car, but this set has two baggage cars and no coach.
B. Ehrlich Collection

ABOVE Bing *Kaiser* coach, 1898 (J); Bing station, 1898 (K); Bing sleeping coach, 1902 (H); Bing dining coach, 1902 (H); Bing newspaper kiosk, 1902 (I) ; Bing express locomotive, 1898 (K); Pride Lines reproduction lamp, current (B)
In direct competition with Märklin at the turn of the century, the firm of Bing matched its rival in quality and was superior in design, but could never compete with Märklin's enormous variety, particularly in the range of accessories. Facing failure in the luxury market, Bing began to concentrate on mass production, and it is interesting that none of the high-quality pieces pictured above is in the 1904 catalogue. The Bing station is larger than most

Märklin stations and appeared in both hand-painted and lithographed versions. The extraordinarily elaborate newspaper kiosk is painted and decorated with transfers showing book titles in English, French, German and Spanish. *P. Carlson Collection*

Little is known in detail about Märklin's exhibit at the 1891 Leipzig Toy Fair except that it was in the form of a figure-of-eight and that it was an enormous sensation. The great significance of the Leipzig Fair exhibit was not that a new toy train had been displayed but that an entirely new concept in toy trains had been invented – the idea that a toy train was part of a system and not just a single object. As a system, there was no limit to its extent, and it could grow indefinitely. This was the aspect of toy trains that Märklin grasped immediately and, applying the thinking that sold so much dolls' house furniture, began to supply an endless variety of accessories to embellish the new railway system. Märklin tried to provide everything that a budding railway tycoon would need in order to run an efficient railway. There were stations, ranging from small country halts to grand terminuses, complete with patient crowds of plaster passengers and helpful officials. There were sheds to keep the passengers dry if it was raining, destination signs, which could be lit at night-time, over-bridges, toilets, signals, buffets, weighing houses and refreshment carts with gargantuan servings of plaster food.

All that was just the station complex, and there was much more out on the line: bridges with lamps, which could be lit at night, tunnels, with giddy mountain paths and ruined castles, signal cabins, cattle pens, engine sheds and marvellously complex level crossings. Points and turntables were added to Märklin's new track layout, so that all the accessories could be arranged to form a complete miniature railway world.

Soon after the introduction of the three gauges, Märklin brought out another gauge. Issmayer and other German manufacturers were doing well with a smaller gauge, and Märklin realized that a new gauge of about 35mm ($1\frac{1}{4}$in) between the rails would be a shrewd addition to the

Plank *Vulkan*, 1895 (H)
One of the countless *Vulkans* produced by this German manufacturer, the example here is intended for running on track with the rails set 65mm apart, a size that Plank called gauge VIII. The tender wheels were made from a special patented pressing and were a feature of the extremely lightweight rolling stock that Plank provided for its not-very-powerful steamers. *Sotheby's, London*

range. The number below I is zero, so this is what the new gauge was named. Because a zero looks like the letter "O", the small gauge became known as gauge O; from then on all additional new gauges were given letter designations – i.e. S, OO, HO, TT, N and Z.

Märklin's invention of the track and gauge system did not go unnoticed by the other German manufacturers nor, indeed, by French manufacturers who were in touch with what was happening in Germany. Schönner adopted the standard gauges I, II and III but added another gauge at 67mm (2½in), which it designated IIA. Bing, Märklin's greatest rival, used the same gauge system as Schönner but used the number IV for the 75mm gauge and III for the 67mm gauge; thus Bing gauge IV was the same as Märklin gauge III, which caused some confusion. Plank was still selling brass "dribblers" in the 1890s, and the gauge it used was quite wide – 65mm – in proportion to the "dribblers'" size. This gauge was Plank's largest and, for some inexplicable reason, was described as gauge VIII. However, it never became a standard.

Carette, typically, took a slightly different approach. It had a motley selection of floor-running steam "dribblers" that had various indeterminate gauges, and it had a range of track-following steamers, which were built to the popular gauge I size, 48mm, and to a larger gauge of 65mm, which Carette called gauge III. Carette also listed a very large 2-4-0 steamer, but, since the gauge was not given and the rails and rolling stock were not available for it, the locomotive might have been intended for technical school demonstrations.

Issmayer continued to manufacture its small 30mm gauge, which was not quite a true gauge O, and added a gauge I to its range. The firm also supplied the entire Carette clockwork range in two non-standard gauges:

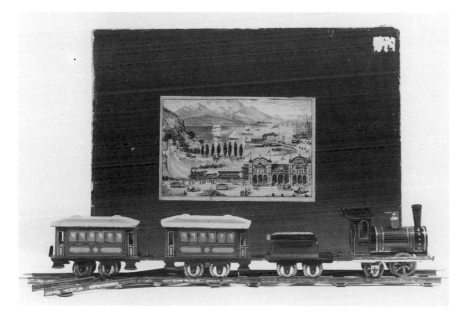

Issmayer train set, 1898 (H)
This lovely little lithographed gauge O set has a locomotive with a Storkleg configuration, which is typical of all early Issmayer production. The picture on the box lid is a masterpiece of evocative art, portraying a vast and complex railway scene in a very charming, toy-like form. *Sotheby's, London*

FAR LEFT Plank *Vulkan*, 1895 (H)
The Plank company always followed an independent course when it came to locomotives, and the spidery, upright Vulkan is very representative of Plank styling. The word "Vulkan" is not of much use for identification purposes because it was almost the only name Plank ever used. This floor-runner has movable front wheels so that it can be set to run in a circle. The design shows considerable British influence, but the light construction, with painted cab and headlamps, is typically German. *B. Ehrlich Collection*

LEFT Carette Storkleg set, 1898 (I)
When the pretty box is opened, the gauge I set inside is surprisingly small, looking more like gauge O than gauge I. In 1898, Carette supplied a wide range of toy trains in different scales – three sizes for gauge I and four sizes for gauge III - but left the gauge O items sub-contracted to Issmayer. The small-sized rolling stock was probably necessary for the underpowered Carette locomotives, which, at this time, were available only as steamers. *Courtesy London Toy and Model Museum*

F.V. train set, 1895 (F); Issmayer station, 1890 (G); Issmayer gauge I train set, 1898 (H)
The little French F.V. set has a non-standard gauge, slightly narrower than gauge O, and the axles are set on a radius, so that only circular running is possible, although the train is intended to run on tracks. The Issmayer train is also a floor-runner with axles on a radius. As originally sold the set did not include a tender, and it is illustrate in this way in the 1898 Carette catalogue. The Issmayer station is an example of the very early use of lithography; there are no tabs, and the station is carefully soldered together, with a hand-painted base, roof and rear wall. *Courtesy London Toy and Model Museum; P. Carlson Collection*

25mm and 30mm, both smaller than gauge O. Issmayer provided Schönner with a 25mm gauge 0-4-0 clockwork train, which came with or without a cowcatcher and some attractive 8-wheeled coaches.

By 1895 gauges O, I, II, III and IV became standard for German manufacturers, and the designations stuck, although gauge O did not appear in most makers' catalogues until c.1900. Other gauges, some smaller than O, some intermediate and some larger than IV, came and went, but none of them seemed to have acquired the dignity of a number or letter. The German firms quickly realized the advantages of having compatible track standards. It meant that a customer with a toy railway system could add to it from the products of any of the German toy train manufacturers. The result was a much larger market for everyone, and a customer of one firm was a potential customer of all the others. Small companies could compete by offering complementary or specialized products and price advantages.

The progress made by the German manufacturers during the 1890s went almost unnoticed by the Americans and British, who continued to produce their outdated toy trains to designs that, in some cases, had been unchanged for decades. In one British list, published c.1900 by R.W. Parks, Model Engineer, Sea Side Road Works, Eastbourne, over fifty different types of brass and tin "dribblers" were described, but the gauge of these locomotives was not given once, even though measurements were included for overall length, boiler diameter, cylinder stroke and driving wheel diameter. Another catalogue, issued in 1897 by John Theobald and Co., 19 Farringdon Road, London, listed 23 different locomotives. Track was for sale, with the diameter given of the circle it made, but not the gauge. Carriages, in four different sizes, were available for running on track, although again, no track size was given. In the United States, there was no standardization of track sizes, and track gauge was defined by the distance between the centres of the two running rails, which were usually metal strips, set on edge in wooden ties.

BELOW LEFT Stevens's Model Dockyard *Thunderer*, 1892 (1)
This brass "dribbler" is a very good example of the British school of locomotive design. As usual with these floor-running locomotives, although expensive and charming, they had a certain crudeness and an antique look about them even when new. This one has lost its chimney but is, in all other respects, complete and in nearly new condition. *Phillips*

BELOW RIGHT Stevens's Model Dockyard *Greater Britain*, 1895 (1)
One of the largest of the British brass locomotives, the rather awkward *Greater Britain* does not have as much period charm as the *Thunderer* from the same maker (left). The wagons are quite rare and are seldom found with these floor-runners, but the tender with this example does not appear to be original. *Sotheby's, London*

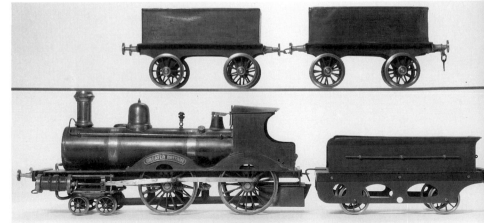

MOTIVE POWER

In Germany during the 1890s, one other area was of major concern: motive power. In the 1870s Issmayer and Hess had developed miniature, but strong, clockwork mechanisms, which could be manufactured comparatively cheaply. Märklin's first locomotives had strong but crude clockwork motors that had neither a governor nor a reverse. Schönner produced no clockwork mechanisms of its own until *c*.1898, while Carette used only steam power, relying on Issmayer for its clockwork trains. Bing's clockwork was the best, and it was capable of powering trains from gauge O up to gauge IV. The largest clockwork was so powerful that gauge IV locomotives were perfectly capable of hauling adults around the tracks, provided the track was strong enough. Early Bing mechanisms had a forward/reverse lever, which shifted gears back and forth, like a car transmission.

By 1895 Märklin was making floor trains with or without clockwork, and clockwork locomotives with or without brakes. The company also introduced a mechanism that would go in reverse as well as forwards, but only one locomotive, in gauges I and II, had both brakes and a reverse. At that time, Märklin manufactured no steamers and no electrics, however.

By 1892 Carette had on display an electric street car that ran on a 2-rail system from dry-cell or wet-cell batteries. Insulation problems hampered the development of 2-rail systems, and Carette's electric railways were limited to a single tram running around in a circle on a single piece of track. By 1898 Carette had produced two different types of 4-wheeled tram and an exotic 8-wheeled tram with open-end platforms. Schönner had an electric 4-wheel tram by 1895, and in its 1900 catalogue was one that took the current from an overhead wire. Plank, too, perhaps as early as 1891, had a 4-wheeled tram, which ran on special tin track and got its power from two wet cells.

The firm that takes the credit for being the first successful American manufacturer of electrically powered toy trains was the obscure firm of

Carlisle & Finch tram, 1899 (H); Carlisle & Finch mining train, 1899 (G)
A small, Mid-western firm, Carlisle & Finch was the first successful manufacturer of electric toy trains in the United States. The trains were usually finished in shiny copper or nickel, and all the frames were made of green-stained wood. The track was made from metal strips, set 2in apart, which happened to be very close to the measurement for gauge II (54mm).
Sotheby's, New York

Carlisle & Finch, located in Cincinnati, Ohio. In 1897 it brought out a 4-wheeled electric tram and followed this in 1898 by an ambitious 8-wheeled inter-urban. These cars ran on the usual American strip rails, which were 2in apart and set into wooden ties. At first a centre rail was used for the electric current, but this was quickly dropped in favour of a 2-rail system, which remained unchanged until the firm stopped making toy trains in 1916. Carlisle & Finch was not originally a mainstream toy manufacturer. The firm made electric motors, searchlights, dynamos and, to round off its line, a few electric novelties. The electric trams were unexpectedly popular and encouraged the company to expand its range by adding steam outline locomotives and rolling stock.

Although Carette's electric street car had appeared in 1892, it is generally accepted that the first electric train sets to appear in Europe were produced by Märklin. Beginning with the ubiquitous 4-wheeled tram, Märklin moved quickly into the new field, and, in 1898, was the first European manufacturer to have an electric drive for its steam outline locomotives. However, in a typically Märklin move, clockwork mechanisms were thoughtfully provided as alternative power for the trams. The electric track had three rails, with the centre rail conducting alternating current, a design that became standard throughout the international toy industry and a system that Märklin still uses today. In the early, experimental days, however, the power for the trams could also be transmitted through overhead wires, as in the prototype.

The electric motors manufactured by Märklin were quite substantial and came in a variety of different designs. Some motors had their bearings on the outside of the wheels, carried on cast outriggers, which were fluted so that they resembled connecting rods. Three voltages were quoted in the catalogue: a 4-volt, an 8-volt, and, for the brave, a strong current system described as 110–250 volts.

By the turn of the century Märklin listed three different kinds of motive power: clockwork, steam and electric, available in four different gauges, using original designs, all of which were new and in a continuous state of development. No other manufacturer had such a wide-ranging programme as Märklin; and no other manufacturer had such hard-working designers – they were the most productive in the whole toy industry. The energetic Märklin directorship had clearly taken the lead in the 1890s. The company's technological gambles had succeeded, the extent, variety, and complexity of its range was unequalled and its marketing was worldwide. Successes were exploited and failures were quickly dropped.

Other German manufacturers were forced to compete on Märklin's terms. Yearly changes in designs became standard practice for the German companies, unlike those of the United States, Britain and France, where changes were introduced only slowly and items in catalogues remained unchanged for years. By 1900, any toy company in Germany that could not take the pace was destined for bankruptcy.

Märklin's products were not, however, cheap. The company's ability

Schönner steam floor locomotive, 1892 (G)

Although equipped with flanged wheels, these Schönner locomotives were intended to run on the floor. The example here is missing its chimney and has at least one replacement buffer, but otherwise it seems to be a good specimen. The inclusion of working steam pipes from the steam dome to the cylinders was a persistent Schönner design feature. *Phillips*

to provide a great variety depended, to a large extent, upon cheap, skilled labour aided by an extensive array of generalized machine tools, such as presses and punches. A skilled tinsmith with a soldering iron, a press for embossing, a punch for windows and doors and some bending tools could make the entire range of Märklin stations. Changes and improvements in design carried hardly any cost penalty. The finish, usually lacquer with a heavy protective coat of varnish, was superb, and it was the standard by which all other firms' products were judged.

Rock & Graner, an old established German toy-making firm, added clockwork trains and accessories to its range in 1896 (selling them under the name of R. & G. N.), trying to copy Märklin's methods. But it found it difficult to achieve volume production, and the firm was liquidated in 1904. Bing, Carette, Schönner and Plank all followed Märklin's lead, and today the similarity in style of locomotives and accessories makes it sometimes difficult to tell which company made what. Bing, however, came closest to Märklin in design, finish and range of products.

While Märklin and its competitors produced expensive toy trains, the lower end of the market was largely left to firms like Issmayer and Hess.

Märklin 0-4-0, 1899 (J)
This gauge II locomotive is an 0-4-0, but the trailing wheel is not as large as the driving wheel. The connecting rod between the two wheels is of the "skating" variety, which, in fact, does nothing but allows the wheels to be out of quarter or even to be of different sizes! *Sotheby's, London*

Märklin train set, 1899 (I)
Märklin trains made for pushing around on the floor are extremely rare. This small example is made from parts from the gauge O production, with the very earliest form of coupler. Märklin hardly ever supplied its floor trains with motors, and this set is no exception.
Sotheby's, London

Issmayer *Pacific Express* set, 1895 (I)
A gauge I example of a classic Issmayer set made for sale in the United States, this was probably one of the first toy trains to have sectional tin-plate track. The clockwork motor is surprisingly powerful for a train of comparatively light construction. Similar sets were also available in gauge O, and later trains had enclosed vestibules instead of open-end platforms. The locomotive has been repainted, and, although the tender appears to be missing, many Issmayer sets were catalogued without tenders. *Phillips*

Hess avoided complication and concentrated on lithographed floor toys. Issmayer was more ambitious, and its lithographed clockwork railways were sophisticated as well as cheap. From time to time, Issmayer introduced novelty mechanisms and inventive movements, which found their way into the catalogues of the larger firms. Automatic switching trains, hill-climbing trams, boat-loading systems, stations that rang bells and could reverse trams, automatic ferry boats and other such novelties offered in manufacturers' catalogues were usually from the firm of Issmayer.

Competition among all German manufacturers had become fierce, and the next decade, 1900–10, was to see a shake-out in the German toy industry.

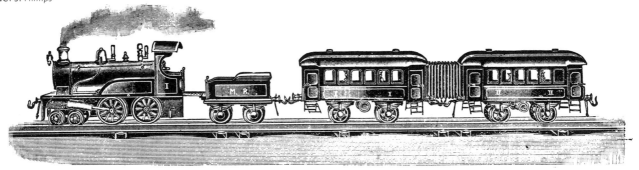

A Bing 1902 gauge I set in the livery of the Midland Railway. The locomotive has no connecting rods and oscillating cylinders.

3
GERMAN PROGRESS AND THE
WORLD MARKET 1900–10

By 1900 public interest in toy railways had become an international craze, and few people could resist the brilliant displays created by Märklin, Bing and the other German toy train manufacturers. A basic toy railway set could be purchased for a modest amount of money; it might have been a circle of track, a locomotive and a couple of coaches, but it was a complete system in itself, and one that could be expanded indefinitely by adding stations, more track, another locomotive, signals, more freight stock and perhaps even an armoured train to go along with the lead soldiers that were also becoming so popular.

The German domestic market was much too small to absorb all the wares on sale from the rapidly expanding German toy industry. German toy train manufacturers had no choice but to become export minded. The American market was the most promising because of the large middle class, the relatively high wages, the strong railway tradition and the large number of German immigrants, who still considered German goods to be the best.

American railways had glamour; railways had won the West, helped subdue the Indians and defeat the South, and they knitted the vast country together. Many American cities owed their existence, and certainly their prosperity, to the railways. American locomotives were like no others with their huge cabs, giant headlamps, thrusting cowcatchers, bells and towering smokestacks – features not found on any European locomotive.

All the German toy train makers produced special trains for sale to the United States from as early as the 1890s. At first, they were primarily floor-runners; Lutz, before its acquisition by Märklin in 1891, catalogued a handsome 4-4-0 with typically American open-platform, 8-wheeled passenger coaches, emblazoned with American eagles. Issmayer made an extensive range of American-styled locomotives and passenger coaches. By 1905 the company's *Pacific Express* coaches appeared in 8-wheeled form in gauge O, gauge I and 30mm gauge, while 4-wheeled American coaches, with open-end platforms and clerestory roofs, and lettered for Boston, New York and Chicago, were made in gauge O and 30mm gauge. Carette catalogued an American Pullman set for its 65mm gauge III, which consisted of a good-looking steam-powered 4-4-0, with two 8-wheeled, clerestory-roofed passenger coaches. Although this train and some small clockwork sets were the extent of Carette's early American effort, Plank offered several sizes of awkward American outline trains for its gauge VIII, including 8-wheeled coaches lettered *Overland Express*.

Märklin Pullman coach and combination, 1912 (l); Carette "Vauclain" Compound, 1905 (M)

The two large, hand-painted Märklin Pullmans make a good match for the Carette gauge I Baldwin Compound, which is almost a scale model. Available only in clockwork or steam, the super-detailed Carette locomotive never had a motor suitable for American toy railways, and, in spite of being one of the most realistic toy trains ever made, it was never a sales success. If it had been, Carette might have made accompanying American coaches, and, if these had been up to the high standard of its British coaches, the resulting train would have been sensational. *P. Carlson Collection*

Bing 0-4-0 set, 1900 (l); Schönner 0-4-0, 1900 (H); Märklin 0-4-0, 1900 (H); Märklin snow-plough, 1902 (H); Märklin American caboose, 1902 (H); Bing crane, 1902 (G); Märklin gas-tank wagon, 1900 (E); Märklin box-tipping wagon, 1902 (H)

This group shows how closely the toy trains from the major manufacturers resembled one another during this period. All the clockwork 0-4-0s in this photograph have thick-spoked, red wheels, dark green paint and gold trim; all the wagons have heavy enamel paint, hand lining and lettering, and cast-iron wheels. Of the many different locomotive wheel arrangements, the 0-4-0 was probably the best for running because there were fewer wheels to derail, and the short wagons allowed the young railway enthusiast to operate interesting trains that were not unreasonably long. *P. Carlson Collection.*

A Bing 1902 gauge O steam-powered locomotive, with a single oscillating cylinder in the cab.

ABOVE Bing tram, 1908 (I); C. Rossignol steam tram, 1902 (H); Märklin New York street car, 1912 (M)

The Bing tram has a gauge O body, but it is fitted with a simplified mechanism, with flangeless wheels for floor running. Part of the body is lithographed and part is hand enamelled, in a curious blend of hand finishing and mass production. This particular tram is considerably over scale for gauge O, and trams made subsequently were much smaller. The Rossignol tram is a supreme example of that maker's artistic approach. The detailing is very delicate, and it is a wonder that any examples have survived. Sold originally with a passenger-carrying trailer car, it is a good model of the little steam tram that used to run through Les Halles in Paris. Märklin trams are rare, and this gauge I, uncatalogued street car, intended for the American market, is among the rarest. None of the examples found in gauge I appear ever to have been fitted with a motor, so perhaps they are the survivors of a small batch of prototype models to test dealer reaction. *P. Carlson Collection*

Schönner devoted a large part of its toy train production between 1890 and 1900 to specifically American designs. Early in the decade it produced an attractive 4-2-4 tank locomotive with a gauge of 85mm. This was a steam-powered locomotive, which ran on rails but only in a straight line. There was not much opportunity for an elaborate railway with this train, nor with its companion, an even more attractive and realistic 4-4-0, complete with an 8-wheeled coach, which could not go around curves; only straight track was sold with the sets. The large 4-4-0s came in two gauges, 67mm and 115mm, and they were in Schönner's catalogue until 1900. A peculiar-looking 4-2-2 tank locomotive, powered by steam (as were almost all of Schönner's American designs), was made in 54mm, 67mm and 90mm gauges. These elaborate, but limited, locomotives were included in Schönner's catalogues for 20 years (1884–1904), and by 1904 they must have seemed very antique indeed.

Schönner's early American range, identifiable by its vast, pierced-tin cowcatchers, was enlarged in the late 1890s by two much more modern designs – a smart, trim, American-type 4-4-0 and a similar 2-2-0 tank engine in gauge I. Both of these locomotives were capable of travelling in a straight line and around curves. In addition to these specifically American locomotives, almost any other Schönner engine was available with a cowcatcher added to it.

Bing had only one American 4-4-0 on offer before 1900, but it was a particularly fine example, with a 3-windowed cab; it was listed in gauges I and II, but none of the firm's early rolling stock seems to have been made specifically to please North American tastes. Issmayer supplied Bing with its gauge O and smaller clockwork 0-2-2s and passenger coaches, which Bing sold in the United States. The sets were equipped with cowcatchers, bells and other American features. Issmayer's small-gauge, finely lithographed trains were certainly popular with its fellow German firms, particularly around the turn of the century. Even Karl Bub sold Issmayer train sets in boxes marked "Karl Bub".

Märklin followed its success at the Leipzig Toy Fair with the production of an extensive American range. It took over the beautiful Lutz American 4-4-0 and shortened it so that it became a 2-4-0. A series of 8-wheeled postal cars and *Eagle* coaches followed, both types with open-end platforms and clerestory roofs. This set was powered by clockwork and ran on gauge II track. The early *Eagle* coaches were quickly replaced by improved, longer versions with a sleeker roof profile, and they sported American shields as well as eagles.

The clockwork locomotives in gauges I, II and III that the German manufacturers exported to the United States were based on American-style prototypes. The steamers, however, were usually modelled on German lines, with bells and cowcatchers added for the American market. In addition to the items that were specifically designed for the United States, German toy train manufacturers also exported their ordinary continental designs. American buyers were not too concerned about the outlines of their toy locomotives, and, in any case, at the turn of

the century, German imports were certainly much better than anything made by the American toy industry.

THE EMERGENCE OF IVES

German domination of the toy train market in the United States was not, however, destined to last. The early years of the 20th century saw the emergence of American toy manufacturers that quickly rivalled the products offered by the German companies.

The most significant of these companies was Ives, the first American firm to manufacture clockwork trains that ran on tracks. Until the firm's factory was destroyed by fire in 1900, Edward and Harry Ives had been major suppliers of mechanical toys and cast-iron trains to the American market. The fire put an end to the old mechanical toy business, which, in any case, was being swamped by German imports. More importantly, the insurance money from the fire enabled Ives to build a brand new

Carette Storkleg train set, 1908 (J)
The gauge I Carette Storkleg has been modified for the American market by the addition of a cowcatcher – otherwise the train set is pure German. The de luxe 8-wheeled coaches are much scarcer than the engine, and it is rare to come across a complete set. Note the difference in roof treatment between the two coaches. The Storkleg is a de luxe model, with fixed cylinders.
Sotheby's, New York

Märklin 0-4-0 steam locomotive, 1902 (M); Märklin 0-4-0 rack locomotive, 1902 (K); Märklin cement wagon, 1902 (D); Märklin beer wagon, 1902 (E); Märklin oil tanker, 1902 (D); Märklin postal coach, 1902 (G)

This group of early Märklin gauge O equipment, all with the wide loop coupler, is in unusually good condition. The steamer (above), which should be united with the tender (below it), is the extremely rare "blow-lamp" locomotive. It uses a very complex method of firing the boiler: fuel is carried in a reservoir in the tender as well as one in the cab roof, and the burner, which is in the cab, shoots flames into the centre flue boiler. (Märklin boilers have a characteristic pudgy shape because they have to hold a hot air tube as well as water.) More complication follows: the steam cylinders drive a centre-crankshaft, which drives internal gears which, in turn, drive the wheels. All this complicated mechanics was expensive, and the "blow-lamp" locomotive did not last long in the catalogue. Another interesting engine is the clockwork rack locomotive. By using a toothed gear wheel and special track, this locomotive was able to ascend and descend steep inclines, and it was often sold with elaborate mountain layouts. The wagons are all rare and desirable, especially the postal coach. *Sotheby's, New York*

factory and equip it with modern machinery. Edward and Harry studied the German products, and, by 1901, the new Ives plant was manufacturing clockwork toy trains and tin-plate sectional track to gauge O standards.

The cast-iron floor trains that had been Ives' main product during the 1890s continued to be produced for at least another fifteen years and directly influenced the evolution of American toy trains, but clockwork was the motive power that Ives understood best, and it was the only motive power the firm used for almost a decade. At first, Ives was content to make close copies of the cheaper German locomotives, usually adopting the 0-2-2 wheel arrangements favoured by Issmayer and Märklin. In fact, the small tin-plate Ives gauge O locomotive of 1901, with its cone smokestack and arched cab windows, looked almost identical to the popular Issmayer product, except that the relative positions of the large driving wheel and small wheel were reversed. The Ives wheels closely resembled Märklin wheels, with their distinctive wedge-shaped spokes, but the most obvious feature copied from Märklin was the shield-shaped trademark. One had to look very closely to recognize the letters "I.M.C." (Ives Manufacturing Company), and Ives continued to use the device until 1905, when it was removed after strenuous objections by Märklin.

The first Ives locomotives produced in the new factory were made up from tin stampings. They had cast-iron wheels and were hand-painted in black and had red or gold decorations. Lithography to decorate the stamped-tin locomotives was introduced in 1904. The locomotives were available in gauge O in five different sizes, although all of them were 2-2-0s. Ives sectional tin-plate track followed standard German practice.

The rolling stock for the Ives line tended to be passenger coaches, and, until 1908, the only freight wagon was an open gondola, which was a direct copy of a Märklin wagon, even to the characteristic green paint with two horizontal stripes.

The first Ives coaches were 4-wheeled, hand-painted copies of Märklin coaches, with cast-iron wheels. In 1903, the coaches were lengthened, and small vestibules were added to each end. In 1904–5 the gothic-style Märklin windows gave way to more conventional ones, and lithographic decoration replaced hand painting. The little tin coaches bore the words "Limited Vestibule Express", a grand title, which took up the entire length of the coach. Also in 1904–5, 8-wheeled coaches were added to the range. These were beautiful vehicles, deliberately designed to be slightly longer than any of the coaches the Germans were making. They were elaborately decorated and also lithographed with the words "Limited Vestibule Express". Interestingly, these early coaches had inside frames for the wheels, which made the coaches look rather old-fashioned and somewhat like the Beggs paper-sided coaches of the previous decade.

In 1904 a new, good-looking and well-proportioned 4-4-0, intended to be the *de luxe*, top-of-the-line Ives train, inaugurated gauge I. This 4-4-0 was a good model of a Baldwin "Vauclain" Compound. Its realism was not to be surpassed until the late 1920s, but its construction was even more significant. The 4-4-0s had cast-iron bodies, similar to the cast-iron floor trains that Ives had manufactured before 1900, and represented a real breakaway from German manufacturing methods. However, gauge I was not expanded very quickly by Ives, and only one 0-4-0 joined the 4-4-0 between 1904 and 1910. A small series of lithographed, 8-wheeled freight rolling stock was brought out in 1906, and by 1910 there were five types of freight wagon available. Rather cheap-looking and never popular, nor even illustrated in the Ives catalogue, they are correspondingly rare today.

The lithographed passenger coaches, first listed in 1904, were much more fitting companions for the high-stepping gauge I 4-4-0. They featured full vestibules and were lithographed with the words "Twentieth Century Limited Express". The lithography was carefully executed, and the simulated wood-panelled sides with decorative scrollwork added a lot of character. The bodies had side openings, with steps but no doors. Unlike the German imports, the Ives passenger coaches had fixed roofs and no interior detail.

Between 1901 and 1910, Ives, with its modern plant, good distribution and value for money, was the German toy train manufacturers' most important American competitor. Just as the American manufacturers had watched developments in Germany, so the Germans followed closely Ives' progress and, although they were not impressed by the American clockwork motors, they were impressed by Ives's cast-iron superstructures, particularly the gauge I Compound.

An American cast-iron floor locomotive with steel coaches. Made in 1902 by the Harris Toy Company, the set measured $40\frac{1}{4}$ in (102cm).

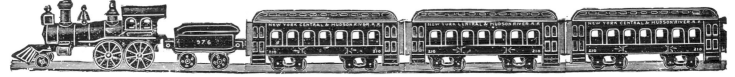

AMERICAN MANUFACTURERS TAKE UP THE CHALLENGE

Elsewhere in the United States, other American firms were starting to manufacture the new train sets. By 1900 Carlisle & Finch (see page 36) was offering quite a nice little range of electrically powered trains. The company offered trams in two different sizes, a mining locomotive with appropriate coal cars and a steam outline 0-4-0 and tender, which came with either 8-wheeled freight rolling stock or 8-wheeled passenger coaches. The passenger coaches were simply lettered "Electric Railway", but the baggage coach bore the elaborate legend "Union Pacific R.R. Baggage Express", which covered even the door. The wheels were mounted on inside frames, in the manner of coaches by Beggs and Ives.

To the Germans, the Carlisle & Finch trains appeared to be pretty crude affairs. The lettering was on paper, which was glued to the sides of the coaches and freight stock. The trams and the coaches had punched-out windows, but windows for the 0-4-0 locomotive were merely printed paper representations, glued on to the cab. All the frames, including those for the locomotives, were made of wood, dyed green. There were good reasons for using wood; its insulating properties, lightness and ease of manufacture were three of them. The lightweight, sheet metal bodies were simply nailed to the wooden frames, while other fittings, such as locomotive steam domes, were turned out of wood. The lightweight construction was necessary because of the low power output of the motor. Later versions of Carlisle & Finch locomotives had proper, punched-out cab windows and embossed or rubber-stamped lettering, the paper overlays having been gradually phased out.

By 1910, 10 years later, Carlisle & Finch added two more trams to its line. One of them was a rather elegant summer car, with rows of seats; the motor was under the floor, and the seats could be turned so that the passengers could always sit facing forward. The steam outline 0-4-0 locomotive and tender had been joined by an 0-4-0 tank locomotive and two 4-4-2 Atlantics. The smaller Atlantic was decorated in the livery of the Pennsylvania Railroad and the larger for the New York Central and Hudson River Line. Both locomotives had excellent proportions and looked very much like their prototypes, but the lightweight assembly system made them appear somewhat flimsy. Although advanced in its use of electricity, Carlisle & Finch was let down by a lack of finish, which varied. The small Atlantic could be supplied completely nickel-plated, together with polished brass passenger coaches, which combined to make a very attractive train. By 1910, the old-fashioned, open-end platform design of the coaches that Carlisle & Finch had continued to produce was not in keeping with the more modern outline of the firm's two Atlantics. A modest number of freight cars, which included two good-looking cabooses, was also available, and all the rolling stock, with the exception of the mining coal cars, was 8-wheeled.

Working along similar lines to Carlisle & Finch in the use of lightweight design was the American firm of Howard. In 1904 the company produced electrically-driven steam outline trains to run on 2in

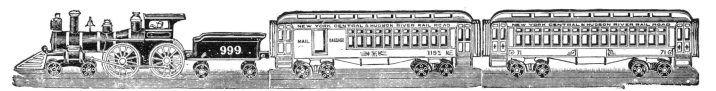

A cast-iron floor train made by the Harris Toy Company; the set measured 42in (107cm).

gauge track, which, by happy accident, was the same measurement as gauge II. Most of its locomotives were ungainly as well as crude, but they did have working electric headlights – not that they helped sales much, as the firm went out of business by 1910! By far the best-looking locomotive produced by Howard was its No. 8, an elegant 4-4-0, which bore the livery of the New York Central Line and carried the number "999".

Another American manufacturer that used 2in gauge was the Knapp Electric & Novelty Co. Starting production of electric locomotives in 1906, the company lasted until 1913, when it was finally put out of business by problems with its difficult strip track, despite having made valiant efforts with sectional track using wooden ties and hollow rail. This was a common problem, and many American manufacturers failed to realize the advantages of the German tin-plate sectional track design, particularly the ease with which it could be assembled and dis-assembled, a feature that made it ideal for temporary layouts. Knapp locomotives, in contrast to those produced by Carlisle & Finch and Howard, employed a heavy cast-iron construction, with working coil springs. The range was limited to a rather ponderous 4-wheeled electric outline locomotive, a well-detailed 0-4-0 steam outline engine, with an 8-wheeled tender, and a tram. For rolling stock Knapp made a few passenger coaches, constructed from wood and metal.

The last, and most important, member of the American "gauge II aristocracy" was Voltamp. The Voltamp Electric Manufacturing Co. of Baltimore was founded by Manes E. Fuld who, as a present for his son, designed an electric railway in 1879. By c.1903 the firm was making locomotives and rolling stock that approached the work of Germans in quality and surpassed most manufacturers in terms of design.

Voltamp developed a heavy iron under-frame with working coil springs, which it used for an attractive 4-wheeled tram with a clerestory roof; the under-frame was also used for a 4-wheeled steeple-cab electric outline locomotive. Another smaller, cast-iron, 4-wheeled bogie was also developed; this could be powered or simply used as a truck. A rather stark 8-wheeled electric outline locomotive with a sheet metal super-structure made use of the bogie, and this locomotive was followed by an 8-wheeled trolley and an exceedingly elegant inter-urban. The non-powered version of the iron under-frame was available for passenger coaches and freight rolling stock. The small items of rolling stock and the caboose needed only one bogie, which did not look out of proportion because of the under-frame's great size and elaborate detail. However, the under-frames looked best under the 18in (46cm) passenger coaches, which stood a good 6in (15cm) high.

Carlisle & Finch train set, 1908 (K)
The No. 34 Atlantic, the smaller of the two Atlantics available, and the caboose and passenger coach are good examples of the 2in gauge trains offered by the small Mid-western American firm of Carlisle & Finch. Although the thin sheet-metal and wooden frame construction look crude to European eyes, the lightweight trains had good insulation properties. Insulation was necessary because Carlisle & Finch pioneered the use of electricity and manufactured electrically powered trains only, designed to run on 2-rail track. The spun-brass wheels had better rolling qualities than the cast-iron wheels used by most European manufacturers. *Courtesy London Toy and Model Museum*

These large Voltamp passenger coaches were constructed from wood and tin plate, and they had beautifully embossed sides, with arched windows and special oval windows for the toilets. The coaches were complete with gas tanks, clerestory windows, handrails and interior detail. The observation coach was particularly striking, and all the coaches had electric lighting as an optional extra.

For an American manufacturer, Voltamp had an impressive range of locomotives. Aside from three different types of trams, there was a 4-wheeled electric steeple cab, which was described as a mining or tunnel motor, and a large 8-wheeled New York Central Line electric outline locomotive, which was equipped with electric headlights, cowcatchers and a bell, but, oddly enough, no pantographs. The firm's steam outline motive power range started with a small, but well-proportioned, 0-4-0 with a 4-wheeled tender. Next in size was a larger 0-4-0 with an 8-wheeled tender. The same cab, boiler fittings and tender were shared with a good-looking 4-4-0.

The two largest locomotives, a 4-6-0 and a magnificent 4-6-2 Pacific,

both with large 8-wheeled tenders, were the finest toy locomotives made in the United States before World War I. The Pacific was a giant machine, weighing 11lb (5kg) and measuring 31in (79cm) overall. The powerful electric motor was quoted as being capable of pulling between 10 and 15 of the large 8-wheeled passenger coaches, and it had an electric reverser, as well as a working headlight and fluted connecting rods.

All the steam outline engines manufactured by Voltamp, except the smallest, had the flaring cylinder chests that were characteristic of the steam Compound design by Baldwin & Brooks, which had so great an impact on the toy railway manufacturers in the United States and Europe that small versions were soon running everywhere.

Voltamp's 6-coupled engines were not equalled by American manufacturers for over twenty-five years. Although both Bing and Märklin built large 6-coupled engines especially for the American market before World War I, they were available only in very small numbers. Voltamp used a heavy enamel finish for its locomotives; this was nicely lined in gold, but the paint had a tendency to flake. Voltamp track was usually of the steel ribbon variety, although a rather clumsy sectional track with hollow rails and wooden ties was also listed. With the exception of one station, which also appears in the Carlisle & Finch catalogue, all the other stations, ticket offices, signals and sundry accessories listed in the Voltamp catalogue were in fact products of either Bing or Issmayer. Voltamp production was limited and oriented toward the adult model train enthusiast rather than the toy market – the catalogue listed all the locomotive parts separately so hobbyists could build their own trains.

Voltamp aimed at the upper end of the American market, whereas Ives's specialty was the mass production of inexpensive train sets. By 1907, however, Ives's virtual monopoly of the cheap end of the American-made toy train market began to be challenged by other American

ABOVE **Bing gauge O train set, 1900 (H)**
Thinking that this train set is by Märklin is a perfectly excusable mistake. The clues that point to Bing are the tender rivets, the thin-spoked driving wheels, the shape of the coach windows and the couplers. In the period around the turn of the century, the similarity between Bing and Märklin products was quite pronounced. *Sotheby's, London*

BELOW **Märklin 0-4-0 train set, 1903 (F)**
This is the most common Märklin train set of the period 1900–10 and the one that turns up most frequently. The engine is an undistinguished gauge I 0-4-0, with German styling, accompanied by a blue first-class coach and a red second-class coach. A brown baggage coach, which is not shown, completes the set. *Sotheby's, London*

manufacturers, notably the Chicago-based firm of American Flyer. American Flyer locomotives were closely patterned after the Ives line and were all cast-iron steam outline 0-4-0s, powered by clockwork. The quality was not up to Ives's standard, but, with selling prices that undercut Ives, they sold well. Less successful than American Flyer was the American Miniature Railway Company, founded in 1907 by ex-Ives employees. Its product line, with cast-iron locomotives, almost exactly duplicated the Ives gauge O range. Various difficulties were encountered, and the firm's meagre production ended after five years.

GERMAN RIVALRY

By 1900 Bing came to the realization that its previous head-to-head competition with Märklin was not going to be successful in the long term. Although at the turn of the century Bing was producing locomotives, rolling stock, stations, and accessories that equalled, or even in some cases bettered, Märklin's in both design and quality, it was not overtaking Märklin in either home or export sales. Mass production had to be the answer, so Bing turned its attention to the mass market: the company planned to offer well-designed products that could be made in greater volume and sold at lower prices than those produced by Märklin.

Most of Märklin's output was of soldered construction, with detail soldered on and then elaborately hand painted. This process ensured a good, solid, high-quality product, but it was costly. Bing decided to develop the type of manufacturing methods that had been pioneered by the Nuremberg makers Issmayer, Lehmann and Hess. These involved printing flat sheets of tin by lithography, punching out the shapes and carrying out the final forming and embossing with presses. The finished pieces were assembled by means of small tin tabs and slots, or by rivets and screws. Since embossing and forming gave strength to the tin, toys could be made lighter and yet still be as strong as the soldered type.

After assembly, the lithographed tin was given a protective coat of varnish, and, if care was taken with the design and printing, the results could look more impressive than anything decorated by hand and at a fraction of the cost. For some toys, like stations, Bing employed a combination of methods. The main structure was soldered and hand painted, while details like doors and windows were lithographed before being attached.

The mass-production methods developed by Bing were successful, and the firm's lead was soon followed by other manufacturers including Carette, Karl Bub and Kraus. However, an initial heavy investment in equipment was necessary as well as a commitment to long production runs, so the "Nuremberg style", as the method came to be known, worked best for large and well-financed firms.

Schönner did not adopt the "Nuremberg style" but experimented with alternative methods, including a finish that consisted of applying large printed transfers over enamel. The firm's American designs between 1900 and 1910 were not successful, even though they included the finest floor-runner of the period – a giant, super-detailed and lithographed American 4-4-0, which was produced in three sizes – and by 1910 Schönner had gone out of business.

Plank, too, was struggling with its awkward steam and clockwork locomotives, and by the end of the decade its train line was much reduced and completely static. Among the quality train makers, Rock & Graner probably came closest to Märklin in design and quality, but was hopelessly outclassed in terms of variety. In the end, the effort was too great, and Rock & Graner, one of Germany's oldest toy makers, went into liquidation in 1904. The shake-out of German toy manufacturers had begun.

Armed with its new production methods, Bing thought carefully about its export strategy and planned its American campaign in detail. The new Nuremberg mass-production methods were ideal for the huge production runs necessary for the American market. Bing planned to lithograph both freight and passenger rolling stock in the liveries of American rail companies. Locomotives were to be lithographed replicas of the ubiquitous Baldwin Compound, powered by clockwork and available as either an 0-4-0 or a 4-4-0.

Gauge I and O were chosen for this new campaign, and following Ives's practice, the rolling stock was to be either 4- or 8-wheeled for gauge O and 8-wheeled only for gauge I. Passenger coaches were to be green for the New York Central Line and red for the Pennsylvania Railroad, and would conform to three basic types: a baggage coach, a full coach and an observation coach with a decorative end platform with a gold railing. In order to simplify production, and, again, following Ives's practice, coaches were to have fixed roofs and no interior detail. The clerestory roofs were to be formed from one piece of metal by means of a deep draw pressing. Tin-plate wheels were to replace cast iron, which improved the rolling qualities. New standards of realism were set in the production of this programme and, for most of its freight stock, Bing made use of the 1903 catalogue issued by the American Car & Foundry Co. of St Louis and New York, a major supplier to the American railways of full-sized rolling stock.

It is interesting to observe how closely Bing followed the A.C. & F. prototypes, shortening and simplifying them but using the same lettering, reporting marks and even exactly the same car numbers as the ones in the catalogue. Thus the Bing New York, New Haven and Hartford boxcar bore number 32001, the B. & O. 165795, the Central Railroad of New Jersey 10205 and so forth. The Hocking Valley gondola No. 4610, the Pennsylvania coal and coke hopper, the Peerless tank car and the American leather tank car were also all in the same A.C. & F. catalogue. The refrigerator cars came from some other source, but the Bing Drovers-style caboose was a slight re-working of the one illustrated for the Ferrocarril de Chihuahua Al Pacifico, re-lettered for the Pennsylvania Railroad. The only other caboose in the A.C. & F. catalogue was a 4-wheeler design, which had already been used by Märklin.

Four Märklin trucks offered by Gamage's at the turn of the century. From the top, an 1895 Holborn brewery van, available in gauges O, I and II; a 1901 circus caravan on a truck, available in gauges O and I; a 1901 furniture van on truck, available in gauges O and I; and a 1902 cistern wagon, available in gauges O and I.

A gauge I steam-powered Storkleg locomotive, made by Bing, c.1902.

While Bing was preparing its American programme in 1904, Ives was in the process of introducing its cast-iron locomotive (see pages 44–5). The advantages of this form of construction and its ready acceptance by American customers did not go unnoticed by Bing. Abandoning its comparatively expensive tin-plate Compounds, Bing brought out a new range of cast-iron locomotives for the American market. These closely followed Ives's designs but had better proportions and cleaner castings. Three different American-type 0-4-0s and one 4-4-0 were supplied for gauge O, and one 0-4-0 and one 4-4-0 for gauge I. The locomotives were very realistic, but they were let down by the use of European-styled 6-wheeled tenders for the 4-4-0s, and, under the cab windows, the letters spelling out "Bing" had been cast into the locomotive. Three lithographed American stations were also on offer, as well as several accessories, such as special American street lamps inscribed "Broadway" or "Fifth Avenue". Other stations and accessories from Bing's European range were also included in the American catalogue, and all the steamers were either German or British in outline, and almost all were in the livery of the British railway companies. Initially, Bing American engines were clockwork only – electrically driven Bing American locomotives were not available until 1910.

Märklin's plans for the American market were not so carefully thought through as Bing's; with a less logical programme, the firm aimed at the top end of the market. Whereas Bing concentrated on two gauges and a balanced programme, Märklin made American trains for four gauges. It even had a non-catalogued "freak", which ran on gargantuan $4\frac{5}{8}$in gauge sectional track. Impossible to use as a toy, it was probably intended as a Christmas advertising centrepiece for department stores. Not only did Märklin offer locomotives for every gauge, it also supplied them with three different types of motive power: clockwork, electric and steam. For the greater part of the years between 1900 and 1910, Märklin's electric locomotives were the only ones available in gauges O and I. Bing was slow to introduce electricity, and steam outline electric-driven locomotives were not listed in any of its catalogues until 1908.

From time to time during the decade, Märklin brought out various American-styled freight wagons, mostly 8-wheelers, although the 4-wheeled caboose was popular. Perhaps the most intriguing examples were the beer cars for Schlitz, Budweiser, Pabst and a few others, all of

BELOW RIGHT A Carette gauge I steam Storkleg locomotive of 1902.

BELOW A 1900 Märklin gauge III clockwork locomotive, with skating connecting rods.

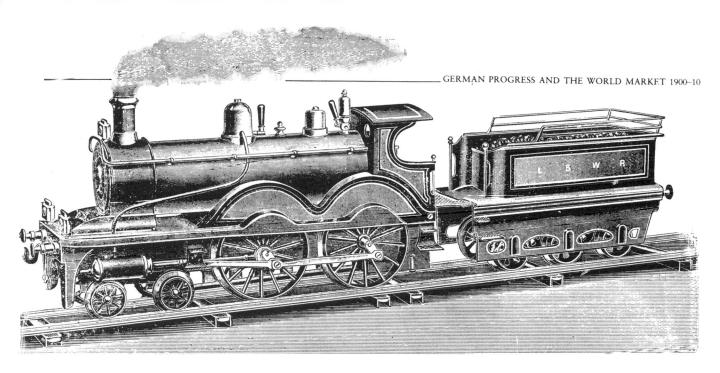

This London and South Western Railway gauge III steam express locomotive by Bing was a *Black Prince* type, 1902.

which were made to different basic designs and painstakingly decorated with rubber stamps, transfers and hand-painted detailing. Märklin American-style locomotives, except for a couple of very early ones, were generally made to German designs, to which had been added cow-catchers, headlights, bells and cabs, with either two or three windows. As conversions, the rather low-slung Märklin engines failed to capture the high-boilered, large-driving-wheel look of American locomotives.

At first, all Märklin's passenger coaches, with the exception of the *Eagle* coaches, were also German in outline. Later in the decade, Märklin produced special American 4- and 8-wheeled coaches with open-end platforms; some were made with end vestibules. Two American-styled stations, similar to Bing stations, were added to the range in 1907. To complement the beer cars, Märklin brought out a series of 8-wheeled freight cars, which were nearly to scale and which included a hopper, a gondola, a San Diego and Arizona tank car, a flat car, two box cars, a Heinz pickle box car and a new large caboose. These new freights were made only in gauges O and I. Their proportions and detail set new standards for toy railway rolling stock, never to be equalled for American-styled gauge I. All in all, Märklin's American products between 1900 and 1910 varied enormously, and the firm's programme was not well coordinated, but its target was the small luxury market found only in a few major East Coast American cities, as opposed to the mass market sought by Bing.

Designs made at Carette were almost always offbeat. Nothing the firm did was odder than its design for a locomotive for the American market. About 1905 the company offered the finest model of a Baldwin "Vauclain" Compound 4-4-0 ever made as a toy. Superbly proportioned and detailed, even down to simulated working valve gear on the clockwork version, it was listed in gauges O, I and II in both steam and clockwork. It was far too fragile and delicate for the

Märklin "RO", 1902 (K)

Märklin's early steam locomotives were totally different in design from the steamers produced by any other manufacturer, and this chunky gauge O "RO" is a typical example. Its most noticeable feature is the large boiler, which was necessary because it contained a fire tube that went through the centre of the boiler from the cab to the chimney. Although being sited at the rear of the burner helped to protect the boiler paint from scorching, Märklin steamers are frequently found with charred cabs. Märklin steam locomotives usually lacked connecting rods between the driving wheels, and what looks like a connecting rod is actually the eccentrically driven valve gear.

American clockwork train market and probably too expensive as well. Because it was virtually a scale model, it was much larger than comparable Bing and Ives locomotives and would have looked out of place on a typical American gauge O or gauge I railway. If it had been made with an electric motor it might have sold to the owners of gauge II electric railways, the Voltamp and Carlisle & Finch market.

The only rolling stock large enough for this locomotive was Märklin's new scale freight cars or the set of hand-painted, 8-wheeled Pullman coaches that Märklin made nearly seven years later. However, since its mechanical reliability was suspect, the locomotive could not be sold on the basis of its performance. It lingered on in various catalogues for years, beautiful but unloved. The failure of Carette's finest effort must have disheartened the Nuremberg firm, because it designed nothing further specifically for the American market. The fact remains, however, that this locomotive was the finest looking American toy locomotive ever made; today it is highly desirable and very rare.

GERMAN PLANS FOR THE BRITISH MARKET

The United States was not the only export market that was of interest to the Germans in 1900. Britain's extensive and well-to-do middle class, which was becoming interested in railways as a hobby, offered a tempting target for the ambitious German toy industry, and the lack of any serious competition from the English toy makers was further inducement. The brass "dribblers" on sale from the small British workshops had changed little in 40 years, and their novelty had worn off.

For several years Schönner, Plank, Carette and Bing had shipped close copies of the cabless "dribblers" to Britain, but during the 1890s the German toy train manufacturers had been making steady improvements in their exports to Britain. Sectional track and rolling stock had become available, locomotives had acquired cabs, and even a few accessories, such as signals, were on sale. Before 1900, however, German manufacturers did not make a serious effort to export to Britain because British locomotives were very distinctive. To sell really well in Britain the Germans would have to supply recognizable British locomotives, and rolling stock in correct liveries.

In Britain itself, two men in particular, W. J. Bassett-Lowke and A. W. Gamage, were interested in good toys, and both had begun to look abroad for suppliers. A. W. Gamage had a large department store in London that was making a name for itself as an emporium where almost anything could be bought, and toys were one of its major specialities.

Märklin station, 1902 (H); Märklin Schlitz beer car, 1906 (M); Märklin Heinz car, 1910 (I); Märklin 4-4-0, 1904 (K); Märklin M.R. train set, 1906 (M) Examples of European gauge O from the 1905 period are rarer than examples of gauge I, and the Märklin assortment illustrated here contains some of the rarest of all. The beautifully made Schlitz and Heinz cars were laboriously hand finished with the aid of some stencils and rubber stamps. The Midland Railway family saloon, which is the end coach on the M.R. train, is the only known example in gauge O, although several exist in gauge I. The M.R. locomotive is basically a later development of the 4-4-0 above it, and both locomotives have a similar mechanism, which utilizes stub axles to carry the rear driving wheels. *P. Carlson Collection*

A gauge I Märklin *La France* locomotive, made c. 1906 in clockwork. The prototype, a French locomotive, was at that time being evaluated by Britain's Great Western Railway.

Wenman J. Bassett-Lowke, who founded his Northampton factory in 1899, had just started up a mail order business, featuring a catalogue filled with interesting toys and scale models. When they visited the 1900 Paris Toy Exhibition, at which all the German toy manufacturers were represented, the sophistication and variety of the German products made a lasting impression on both men.

Gamage placed large orders with Märklin, Bing, Carette and Issmayer for their toy railway systems; these were largely German outline with a few additional American types. However, Gamage wanted to be able to offer British outline trains to his customers. Not merely a store owner, Gamage also ran a huge mail order business, which was the largest and most famous toy outlet not only for Britain but also for the entire British Empire. In 1900 there was a large but untapped market for British outline trains: in 1902, Gamage's offered several different British toy trains for sale, but they were still in the minority compared with the German types. By 1906, the majority of the trains in Gamage's catalogue were British outline, and the number of different types had grown to over 150, many of them exclusive to Gamage's.

The locomotives that Bing supplied to Gamage's for the British market were large, expensive and very bulky. Powered by either clockwork or steam, they were intended for the very top of the market, in contrast to their high-volume, low-cost American trains. At first, Bing

A Bing gauge III 0–4–0, made c. 1906, in the livery of the London & North Western Railway. The 4-wheeled versions of the *Black Prince* type were available only in clockwork.

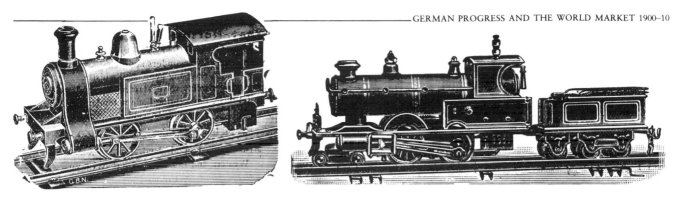

concentrated on the large gauges, leaving gauge O to Märklin, Schönner, Issmayer and Plank. The most common form of Bing locomotive was a gauge I 4-4-0, of which the *Black Prince* was the most famous example. To accompany this range of high-quality locomotives, Bing made special British outline, 8-wheeled passenger coaches with hinged roofs and full interior detail, including luggage-racks and buttoned upholstery. The coaches for the large gauges were hand painted, lined and lettered; later, lithographed versions were made for gauge O.

Four major British railway companies were represented – London & North-Western, Midland, Great Northern and London and South Western – while two basic types of passenger car were available, a coach and a full passenger brake (baggage coach). Bing's heavy soldered, tin-plate construction, with working doors and beautiful finish, was in the Märklin tradition, but it was superior in every aspect to comparable Märklin coaches. Bing's range of British locomotives and coaches was the zenith of the firm's ambitions to compete in the high-quality end of the toy-train market.

Sold under its own name, the Märklin range supplied to Gamage's was extensive but concentrated on gauge O and gauge I. The larger British outline locomotives made by Märklin had the firm's usual ingenious features, but they failed dismally to capture the grace and beauty of British locomotive design. Frankly, the Märklin engines were unusually clumsy and ugly, especially when compared with those produced by Bing. Although the awkward, chunky styling had an undeniable appeal, especially in the smaller gauges, Märklin's gauge III, 75mm, was not only clumsy but under-detailed; the specially designed

ABOVE LEFT A Bing steam tank engine in the style of the London & North Western Railway. Made c.1906 in gauges O and I, the design continued in Bing's range up to the mid-1920s.

ABOVE This gauge O Märklin London & North Western steam locomotive of 1906 has an unusual articulated arrangement for the tender wheels.

Bing L.S.W.R. 4-4-0, 1903 (K)
The Bing gauge II London and South Western Railway 4-4-0 is one of the variations on the popular *Black Prince* type. This example is in very good condition for a steamer; it has a painted boiler and steam dome, although later models had gun-metal boilers and polished brass steam domes. The large, square headlamp is original and is much rarer than the locomotive itself because almost all of the headlamps have been lost. *Sotheby's, London*

Bing L.N.W.R. *Jupiter*, 1904 (J) ; Bing L.N.W.R. passenger coach, 1904 (H); Märklin station, 1909 (I); Märklin lamp, 1904 (G)

The handsome Märklin glass-roofed station and rare hanging lamp are the perfect accessories to display the fine lines and gleaming finish of the Bing London & North-Western Railway *Jupiter* and passenger coach in this period gauge I piece. The coach is an example of the high-quality, hand-enamelled coaches Bing made to accompany its top grade locomotives. For some unexplained reason, Bing coaches of this period are much rarer than the locomotives, and gauge I coaches are even scarcer than coaches in gauges II, III and IV. *P. Carlson Collection*

INSET Bing L.S.W.R. 4-4-0, 1904 (K); Bing L.N.W.R. *Black Prince*, 1903 (K); Bing G.N. *Stirling* Single, 1904 (K); Bing M.R. 4-4-0, 1903 (K)

The superiority of Bing locomotives between 1902 and 1905 is well demonstrated by this group of gauge II locomotives. These high quality, well-proportioned models were made in five different gauges, and for up to five different railway companies, although the blue Caledonian Railway livery, not shown here, was not available in every gauge. Besides these top-grade locomotives, Bing manufactured a host of lesser models, 4-4-0s, Singles and 0-4-0s in clockwork and steam, all specially designed for the British market. *P. Carlson Collection*

gauge III locomotives and coaches did not appear in the Gamage's catalogues for more than a couple of years, which means that any survivors are extremely rare today.

Many special trains were designed and sold exclusively through Gamage's and did not appear in any other catalogue. Consequently, no full listing of the products provided by Bing, Märklin, Carette, Issmayer, Schönner and other German makers can be made without reference to Gamage's catalogues. Fortunately, a few of the old Gamage's catalogues have been preserved and reproduced in facsimile. (See Bibliography, pages 156–8.)

The remarks about exclusive models and catalogue listings also apply to Bassett-Lowke. W.J. Bassett-Lowke is usually thought of as the first Englishman to recognize the quality of the German toy trains and to commission special British designs, but the credit must be shared with A.W. Gamage. Certainly the volume of sales through Gamage's was much more significant to the Germans than the relatively new, and still small, Bassett-Lowke catalogue.

W.J. Bassett-Lowke was a young man who had come up with the idea of issuing a mail order catalogue of high-quality toys, scale models and parts for model locomotive enthusiasts. The first catalogue, featuring photographs of the models stuck in by hand, was sent out in 1899, and it met with an enthusiastic response. By 1904, the Bassett-Lowke catalogue was a hefty 252-page volume and, by 1906, it had to be published in sections, one of which was in French.

In 1902, almost all the German toy firms were exporting to Britain and all of them had at least one British outline train in their lists. Märklin was Gamage's principal train supplier, concentrating on the cheaper sets, while Bing took care of the high-quality end of the market, a reversal of the firms' relative positions in the United States. Bing, on the other hand,

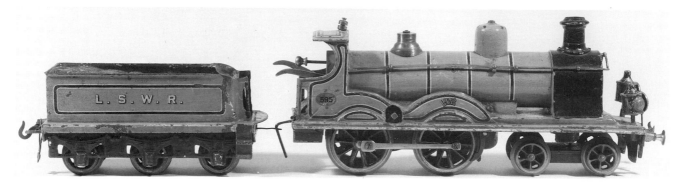

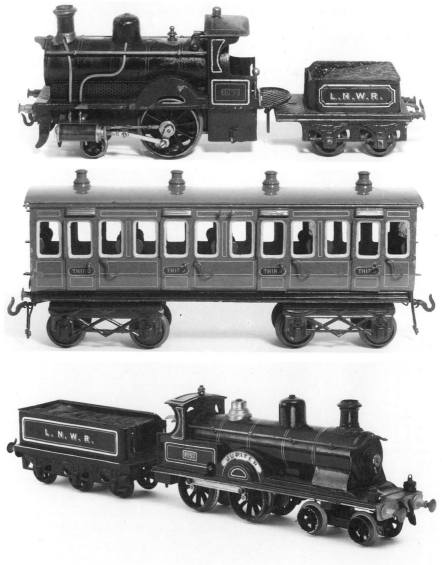

Bing L.S.W.R. 4-4-0, 1902 (l)
The London and South Western
Railway colours of pale green, reddish-
brown and black would enhance the
looks of any locomotive, and this gauge I
4-4-0 is especially attractive. The
hideous lamps on the front belong on a
trackwork turnout. *Sotheby's, London*

Bing L.N.W.R. Storkleg, 1902 (G)
The gauge I, British-styled Storkleg is a
satisfying example of Bing design. It is
also an example of how hard the
Nuremberg manufacturer was trying to
please the British market. This
locomotive has several advanced
features, including a reversing
mechanism, fixed cylinders, double-
acting valve gear and a steam exhaust up
the chimney. *Sotheby's, London*

Bing G.N.R. gauge III coach, 1904 (l)
Large, heavy and beautifully detailed,
Bing made these coaches in four gauges
and decorated them in the liveries of
four different railway companies. They
featured turned-brass door handles,
complete interior with buttoned
upholstery, luggage racks and iron
wheels; each one was hand painted. It
was the finest coach series that Bing
ever made. *Sotheby's, London*

Bing *Jupiter*, 1902 (J)
The Bing gauge I *Jupiter* is in almost mint
condition, with no paint chips on the
steam dome, and it is shown complete
with the correct headlamps. L.N.W.R.
clockwork *Jupiters* were made in many
different variations, but the 1902 4-4-0
with the small cab is considered the
most elegant. *Sotheby's, London*

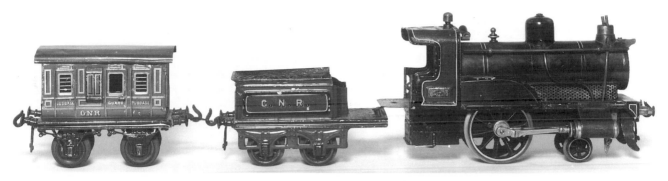

Bing G.N.R. Storkleg, 1905 (F); Bing G.N.R. 4-wheeled passenger brake, 1905 (B)

By 1905, Bing's 4-wheeled coaches were largely lithographed. Because the printing could incorporate far greater detail, the newer coaches were visually superior to the older, hand-painted ones. This gauge I Storkleg has a nice painted boiler, but the chimney is missing. *Sotheby's, London*

Bing M.R. gauge I 0-4-0, 1905 (E)

Bing's lithographed 0-4-0s were made in large numbers, and examples are not hard to find today. Although these were locomotives designed for mass production, they have pleasing lines and, with their shining brass domes, are very acceptable in any collection.
Sotheby's, London

Bing G.N.R. 0-4-0, 1905 (D); Bing oil tanker, 1905 (B); Bing G.N.R. passenger brake, 1905 (B)

The very cheap Bing gauge O lithographed locomotives had the marvellous ability to suggest detail where there actually was none. The splashers over the driving wheels are simply printed on the boiler; the cylinders are there, but the piston rods and connecting rods are not. There is, however, a whistle, the chimney has a cap, there is a polished brass dome, there are buffers and the driving wheels are heavy lead castings, so in some respects, this is a *de luxe* cheap locomotive. The oil tanker is soldered, painted and lettered with rubber stamps, but the brake is tabbed and lithographed. *Sotheby's, London*

was the major supplier for Bassett-Lowke, providing a full range of trains from the cheap sets to the most expensive locomotives.

Carette supplied both Gamage's and Bassett-Lowke. In an effort to gain a foothold in the high-priced, quality market, it produced three extremely heavy, very expensive steam locomotives and made extensive use of iron castings. The rather awkwardly interpreted gauge III 4-2-2 Great Northern Railway *Stirling* Single was, nevertheless, an impressive locomotive with a superb finish. The handsome Great Eastern Railway 4-4-0 *Claude Hamilton*, was listed in gauges I and II, while the third of these heavy steamers was a rather ugly London and North Eastern Railway 4-4-0 bogie express in gauges I and III. These locomotives were listed in both Gamage's and Bassett-Lowke's catalogues until the end of the decade, together with the American "Vauclain" 4-4-0. They were probably not a sales success, because Carette produced no more large-gauge engines, turning instead to lithography and mass production.

Carette's gauge I *Claude Hamilton* was more expensive than either Märklin's gauge III or Bing's gauge IV *Black Prince*. Schönner's monster

Bing L.S.W.R. 0-4-0, 1905 (F); pair of Märklin "exploding" coaches, 1904 (each coach (J); Märklin "exploding" baggage wagon, 1904 (K)
The gauge I 0-4-0 is a standard Bing lithographed locomotive, inexpensive but very attractive. The Märklin coaches are hand painted in a more elaborate finish than usual, and their roofs have an additional boss because they are the very rare "exploding" coaches. Held together by a large central spring, the coaches "explode" when the train is bumped, and the extra long buffer releases a spring. The idea was apparently too gruesome for most buyers because hardly any exist today. *Sotheby's, London*

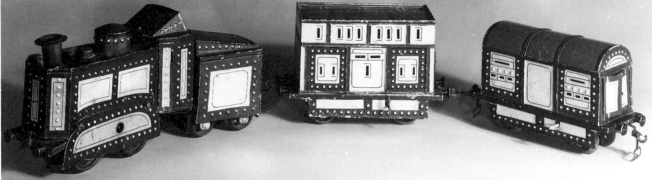

Märklin armoured train, 1904 (M)
Armoured trains, inspired by those used in the Boer War (1899–1902), appeared in gauges O, I and II, and there is evidence that some uncatalogued models were made for Märklin gauge III (75mm). Despite their rather crude, square-cut looks – a feature they share with the prototype – they are avidly sought by collectors. Two additional cars complete the set: an open car for soldiers and a cannon car, which could be pushed ahead of the locomotive and used to clear the tracks by firing cap guns, activated from the rails. *Sotheby's, London*

A cheap Carette gauge O clockwork set of 1906; the locomotive and coaches were probably manufactured by Issmayer.

Plank M.R. Storkleg, 1904 (F); Carette G.N.R. passenger brake, 1906 (B)
For this gauge I locomotive, Plank forsook the usual *Vulkan* and substituted *Union*. Plank locomotive design had arrived at this point by 1904,

and there was to be little further change until the company went under in the 1920s. The Carette passenger brake is a peculiar little coach, of vaguely continental inspiration, which was made in large numbers and had the

virtue of being extremely strong. Some versions had rudimentary interiors, complete with 2-dimensional lead passengers. *Sotheby's, London*

LEFT Märklin L.N.W.R. gauge II coach, 1903 (I); Bing L.N.W.R. gauge II passenger brake, 1904 (H)
Two German coaches are shown here, both purporting to be representative of London & North-Western Railway rolling stock. The Bing coach is typically British with its arc roof, whereas the Märklin one is a typical German vehicle painted for the L.N.W.R. Both examples have hinged roofs and complete interiors. The Märklin coach has a full load of rather sooty plaster passengers, highly prized by collectors. However, for those who cannot get originals, plaster replicas are readily available. *Phillips*

ABOVE Carette N.E.R. 4-4-0, 1906 (J)
A gauge III heavy express locomotive, one of a trio, was made by Carette for the luxury end of the British toy train market. Cast iron was used extensively in the construction, and the cab sides and splashers, as well as the frame, are all castings. To accompany this locomotive, Carette made a lithographed coach and passenger brake

...in full London and North Eastern Railway livery. Lithography, which is more suited for mass production, was an odd choice for what must have been an extremely limited market. *Sotheby's, London*

A 1902 clockwork gauge O 0–6–0, which Märklin interpreted as an 0–4–2.

Carette for Bassett-Lowke water tower (H); Bing signal house (A); Märklin British station (K); Bing destination sign (B); Bing street lamp (B); Bassett-Lowke turntable (G)
This group of accessories is primarily British in outline, but everything was made in Germany. The Bassett-Lowke turntable, with its massive iron side castings, is definitely German, but the particular manufacturer is not known – it might possibly be Carette. The handsome water tower is a classic example of Carette lithography and has dozens of signs advertising various British products. The Märklin station has signs too, but these are painted on, using stencils. On the back of the station is a very large sign for Gamage's, listing several categories of the store's goods. *Phillips*

Bing signal gantry, 1908 (D); Bing crane, 1905 (C); Märklin M.R. open wagon with *Bremserhaus*, 1907 (E); Märklin M.R. goods van, 1907 (F); Märklin G.N.R. sleeping car, 1907 (G); Bing for Bassett-Lowke L.N.W.R. *Bowen-Cooke* tank, 1912 (G)
The giant Bing signal gantry is the right scale to set off this superb assortment of Bing and Märklin gauge II equipment. The two Märklin goods wagons are seldom found with British railway lettering, and the goods van is in a special gold and lake livery, done only for the Midland Railway versions. The Midland Railway sleeping car is one of Märklin's most elaborate coaches and is basically a German express coach painted in G.N.R. colours. The Bing 4-6-2 tank is an impressive locomotive, which was made exclusively for Bassett-Lowke in gauge II only. *Phillips*

Carette G.N.R. *Stirling* Single, 1902 (M)
One of a small series of three very heavy and *de luxe* locomotives that Carette made for the British market, the Single was made only in gauge III and has a cast-iron frame. These impressive locomotives are completely out of character with the balance of Carette's output, and they represent an unsuccessful attempt to enter the British luxury toy train market. *Christie's, London*

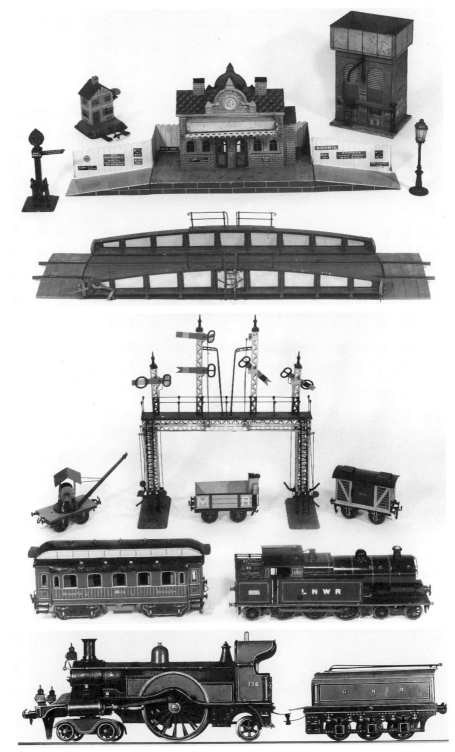

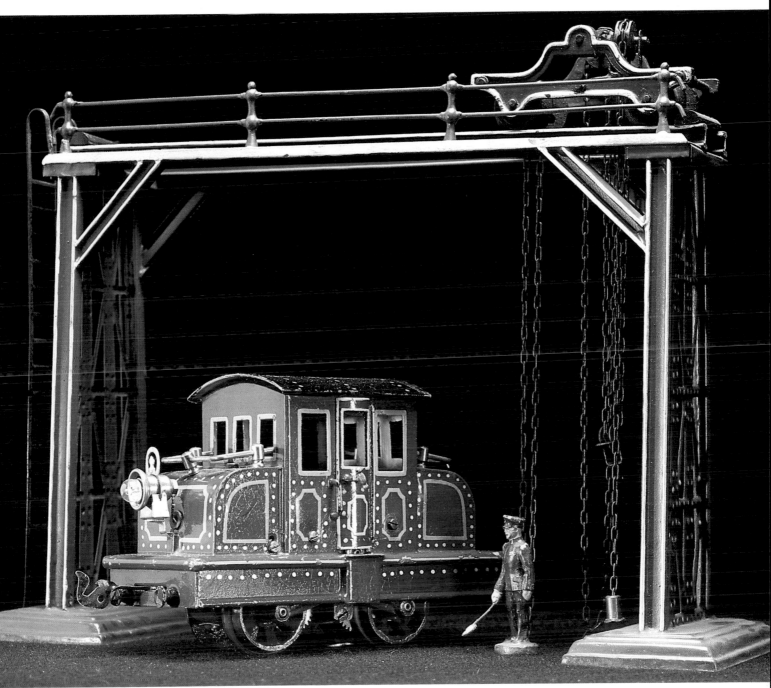

Märklin Central London Railway electric, 1906 (M); Märklin gantry crane, 1906 (I)
The Central London Railway, part of London's underground railway system, provided the prototypes for Märklin's early 4- and 8-wheeled electrics. The electrics were available in gauges O, I and II, although, it is rumoured, a few gauge III versions were also made. The 8-wheeled locomotive was almost entirely a freelance design. The gauge O example shown under the elaborate and fully working gantry crane is almost certainly a high-voltage model.

Bing gauge IV Storkleg, 1902 (K)
This compact locomotive was the largest of Bing's Storkleg series, and it had refinements such as fixed cylinders, headlamps and reversing gear. The very large Bing gauge III and IV Storklegs were always Germanic in outline, even though they were sold in France, Britain and the United States. *Phillips*

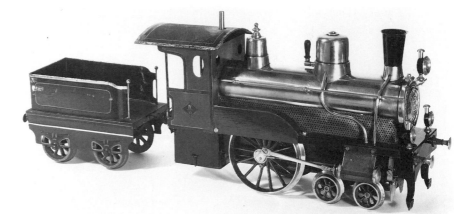

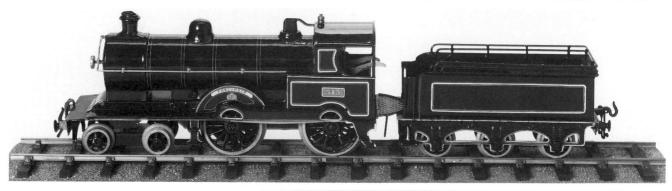

ABOVE Bing for Bassett-Lowke L.N.W.R. *Precursor*, 1905 (G)
The *Precursor* was the most successful of a trio of Bing engines done as scale models for Bassett-Lowke, and it was a remarkable effort compared with what was on the market at the time. This mint gauge I example was never run and has spent its entire life in a glass case. *Phillips*

Carette Storkleg, 1907 (F)
Carette's gauge I Storklegs were tidy little locomotives, but their simple oscillating cylinders and unvarying German design always put them at a disadvantage compared with Bing's more adventurous products. A few *de luxe* Storklegs were made with fixed cylinders and valve gear. *Sotheby's, London*

gauges III and IV engines were even more highly priced and correspondingly unsuccessful. There was a limit to how much a British buyer was prepared to pay for a "toy" train. Interestingly, the British market was unlike either the continental or American markets. Buyers in the United States or on the continent were satisfied with a very limited choice and were not particularly loyal to any one railway company. Customers in Britain, on the other hand, were great railway enthusiasts and liked to see their favourite railway running in miniature. Varieties of locomotives and different railway styles intrigued them as well, and they looked to the toy and model suppliers for a corresponding range. Gamage's and Bassett-Lowke rose to the challenge.

By 1902, and having been in business for only three years, Bassett-Lowke had built up a selection of 43 different locomotives, every one made in Germany. Bing was responsible for the great majority of them, and the 15 British outline models were all by Bing. Gamage's listed 61 different locomotives from Germany and a further five of British manufacture. Eight of Gamage's German imports were British outline, with the balance being divided between German and American styles. Five of the British locomotive types came from Bing, and they were easily the most impressive trains in Gamage's line-up in 1902.

A "decapod", which was patterned after a British experimental locomotive that had 10 driving wheels. For its gauge I and II locomotives, Märklin reduced the number of driving wheels to six, which, with the four leading wheels, still gave a total of 10 wheels. For its gauge O range Märklin reduced the mighty "decapod" to a mere 0–4–0 tank engine. Illustrated here is a 1906 clockwork version made for Gamages.

By 1906, the pace in the British market was feverish and most of the locomotives imported into Britain were British outlines. Gamage's still relied primarily on Märklin for the bulk of its imports, but almost every important German firm was represented in Gamage's catalogue for that year. An unbelievable 152 different locomotives from six different German manufacturers were catalogued. Native British products were down to three examples. Although Märklin was still Gamage's major supplier, the locomotives supplied by Bing were the most expensive and certainly the best looking. Bing was better represented in Bassett-Lowke's 1906 catalogue, which listed 154 different, German-made locomotives, with the majority by Bing. Continental and American types were down to a mere handful, overwhelmed by the flood of British outline trains. After Bing, Carette had the second largest group of locomotives in the Bassett-Lowke catalogue in 1906, with Märklin's products a distant third.

Although Gamage and Bassett-Lowke were merely retailers and distributors, their knowledge of British railway design and their influence over the market was responsible for the initiation of many of the new trains. It has been claimed that Bassett-Lowke was the initiator of the design for the famous *Black Prince* series of Bing 4-4-0 steam locomotives in the four largest gauges. Since this locomotive first appeared in 1900, however, when the small Bassett-Lowke firm had been in existence for only a year, it seems much more likely that this was entirely a Bing effort, especially since the design was not exclusive to Bassett-Lowke and was also catalogued by Gamage's and Clyde Model Dockyard, among others.

**INSET Carette S.E.C.R. rail coach,
1909 (K); Carette S.E.C.R. motor coach,
1907 (I)**
Although made with either steam or
electric motors, and beautifully
lithographed in the livery of the South-
Eastern and Chatham Railway, the
Carette railcars, in both gauge O and
gauge I, were not good sellers. This was
a disappointment to the German firm,
which had obviously tooled up for mass
production. Today, these railcars are
very rare, and the lithography is usually
badly burnt by the steam motor. The
gauge I rail coach illustrated is in almost
unique, undamaged condition. *Courtesy
London Toy and Model Museum; Torrey Collection*

Märklin Rocket, 1907 (M)
Historical models by major toy
companies are not common because
they are hard to integrate into an
everyday railway, and since children
are not very interested in history, sales
are low. Judging from the numbers that
exist, the sales of Märklin's gauge I
Rocket must have been very poor
indeed. Only the occasional adult would
have been interested in a train that
looked like a primitive "dribbler".
Märklin had tried hard, and there are
three wagons, counting the tender,

which are unique to the Rocket,
although the yellow coach is merely a
standard production item with the roof
left off. Since most serious collectors
today are adults, things have changed,
and the Märklin *Rocket* is notorious for
having set the record price for a toy
train sold at auction – £28,050
(approximately $39,000) on the hammer
in May 1984. *Sotheby's London*

Carette's *Lady of the Lake* is a far more likely candidate for the distinction of being Bassett-Lowke's first commissioned locomotive. This was a clever re-working of a basic, but well-proven, Storkleg design into a reasonable replica of a Webb-designed L.N.W.R. 2-2-2, a locomotive of considerable charm and distinction.

The willingness of the Germans to create exclusive designs for the British market led Bassett-Lowke and, to a lesser extent, Gamage's, to be regarded as manufacturers as well as retailers, especially as the German trademarks and signs of corporate identity began to vanish from products exported to Britain. Consumer loyalty to individual manufacturers, which sold so many toy trains in the United States, became blurred, and Bassett-Lowke began to create a unique product line that had a distinct Bassett-Lowke look but that was, in fact, the output of several different manufacturers, most of them German. Henry Greenly, W.J. Bassett-Lowke's great friend and chief designer, had visited the Bing factory in 1901 and quickly realized that, given sufficient direction, the German toy industry could produce very sophisticated trains for the English market. The great German toy industry became a sub-contractor to Bassett-Lowke and Gamage's, and products that were exclusive to the two British firms and sold under their trademarks were actually created by Bing, Carette, Märklin, Schönner and Issmayer.

The designs commissioned by Bassett-Lowke tended to be more and more scale models rather than just toy trains, and by 1907 the toy train sets had begun to disappear from the Bassett-Lowke catalogue as the scale model programme began to gather momentum. By 1910 Bing scale models had proved superior to efforts by both Märklin and Carette, and from then on Bassett-Lowke looked to Bing for the supply of almost its entire new scale model range. Carette's highly detailed lithography had secured it the position of sole supplier for the new Bassett-Lowke passenger coaches and rolling stock.

When sub-contracting or commissioning specially designed products, Gamage's, on the other hand, remained loyal to Märklin, and several large Märklin locomotives were designed to sell for prices that undercut the line Bing produced for Bassett-Lowke. Bing and Carette were also Gamage's sub-contractors, but the top end of the line came to

Pair of Bing wagons lits coaches, 1909 (each coach C)
The Bing 8-wheeled lithographed coaches were made in large quantities over a 20-year period. Although the coaches are charming and well made, their price is usually reasonable because there are so many around. This gauge O pair is in average condition, although the baggage-postal car appears to have a pair of later bogies. *Christie's, London*

be dominated by Märklin's locomotives. A brilliant new series of Märklin passenger coaches and freight wagons, all employing very high-class lithographic decoration, began to appear on the market in 1910 from Gamage's. This new rolling stock marked a change in Märklin's manufacturing methods and underlined the German firm's intention to modernize and become more competitive.

At the end of the decade, Bassett-Lowke and Gamage's were still Britain's two major toy train retailers. The new Bassett-Lowke products were designed with the serious, adult enthusiast in mind, a breed of train buyer appearing in England in increasing numbers. Gamage's approach was broader and its range encompassed cheap train sets for children as well as expensive steam scale models for adults. However, Gamage's and Bassett-Lowke were not the only firms selling toy trains in England, although they are the best known because of the survival of many of their extensive catalogues.

By 1910 every town in England had toy shops that stocked lithographed train sets by Bing, Carette, Karl Bub, Issmayer and Märklin. All these firms, including by that stage Märklin, were producing cheap and colourful sets, using the Nuremberg methods of lithographed sheet tin and tab construction. Different trains were made for every small price increment and in the liveries of at least four different British railway companies. The variety was enormous but the sales were undoubtedly high enough to justify the cost of lithography, cutting, punching and embossing – all processes with a high initial outlay that had to be recovered by volume sales. Although Märklin was Gamage's chief supplier, Bing and Carette had a larger share of the overall British

TOP Bing G.N.R. train set, 1908 (E)
The small Bing lithographed gauge O train sets were produced in huge numbers. They were well made and reliable runners, providing plenty of excitement and not taking up much room. This locomotive is suffering from an indifferent repaint. *Phillips*

ABOVE LEFT Bing L.N.W.R. 4-4-0T, 1904 (G)
Bing tank locomotives were very popular, and smaller 0-4-0T variations in both gauge O and gauge I were continued well into the 1920s. A super-detailed version in the livery of the L.N.W.R. was built especially for Bassett-Lowke. *Sotheby's, London*

ABOVE RIGHT Märklin M.R. sleeping car, 1908 (I)
The gauge II 8-wheeled coach series by Märklin is very impressive; however, with few exceptions, most of the coaches are German types, painted to resemble various prototypes. The coach illustrated here is typical of this Märklin practice, and, although it is painted for the Midland Railway, it does not look much like anything that ran over M.R. rails. *Sotheby's, London*

A Märklin gauge I Great Northern Railway clockwork 4-4-0, with a very rare 8-wheeled tender.

An extremely large gauge III North Eastern Railway express steam locomotive made by Carette mainly from iron castings in 1905.

PREVIOUS PAGES Märklin goods shed, 1904 (H); Märklin P.L.M. *coupe vent*, 1908 (M); Märklin signal, 1904 (D); Märklin water pump with lamp, 1904 (I) This busy railway scene is a good example of how well the Märklin hand-painted accessories complimented one another and of how well Märklin succeeded in enlivening plain, unembossed surfaces with interesting and artistic representations of bricks, timbers, rivets, tiles and so forth. The gauge I *coupe vent* is a loose interpretation of a Maffei 4-6-0, which was built for the P.L.M. in the decade before 1910. In providing a French locomotive, Märklin remained loyal to German interests by following a prototype that was manufactured by a German locomotive firm. In spite of the German origins, French collectors rate the *coupe vent* above any other toy train.

market, and their bright and cheerful train sets were available everywhere.

GERMAN TRAINS FOR FRANCE
France did not seem to attract the German manufacturers in the same way that Britain and the United States had done, even though, as a market, it was geographically close and relatively easy for the Germans to exploit. At the end of the 19th century French toy locomotive styling was not so very different from German styling, but the finish and construction of the German trains were superior to anything French. F.V., Charles Rossignol and, later, S.I.F. (La Société Industrielle de Ferblanterie) had quickly adopted the German sectional tin-track system and the idea of a steadily growing railway empire, but, although their small trains had considerable charm, they were still inferior to the German products in terms of both quality and quantity.

Models based on French prototypes were not introduced at first, however, probably because of the similarity between German and French styling. Bing and Carette did not make any of their expensive, large locomotives especially for the French market. Towards the end of the 19th century, Schönner had established a close working relationship with the old French firm of Heller & Coudray and made many special designs for it, and in a last fling before Schönner went out of business in 1906, it made a huge P.L.M. (Paris–Lyon–Mediterranée) Railway *Coupé Vent* 4-4-0 steamer. Märklin was the only German manufacturer that made an effort to provide a group of special French outline locomotives, although these, at first, were patterned after the P.L.M. *Coupé Vent* locomotives made for the French railways by the German locomotive firm of Maffai.

Märklin monopolized the top end of the French market. Encouraged by its success, it opened its own retail outlet in Paris, and special French trains began to appear in its catalogues. There were several versions of the wind-cutting P.L.M. *Coupé Vent*, available in all gauges, as well as special French coaches and wagons, and even a rather odd coach for transporting prisoners. However, the French Märklin products between 1900 and 1910 were rather "hit-or-miss" affairs and all of them are very rare today.

At the luxury end of the market there was no serious competition from French manufacturers, indicating that the market was quite small and could be satisfactorily supplied by Märklin's stock products and some British outline trains, occasionally decorated with special French paintwork. The absence of German interest at the cheaper end of the market was an opportunity for French firms like S.I.F., which later became J.E.P. (Jouets de Paris), and Rossignol to produce low-price, French-style trains using Nuremberg methods. Both companies made a large variety of lithographed train sets, usually colourful, toy-like and rather idiosyncratic. Because the French manufacturers were primarily interested in competing with the Germans in the French market, very few of their sets were exported; thus today, French trains of this period are seldom found outside France. Clockwork was the motive power most favoured by the French manufacturers, although electricity was used occasionally. Steam was almost never used.

GERMAN TRAINS FOR GERMANY

For the home market, the German toy train makers all produced graduated product lines of German outline locomotives and rolling stock. Much greater emphasis was placed on accessories for the home market than any other market, and the number and variety of German stations, lamps, signals and so on was astonishing. German customers were interested in more than just a train set for children; they wanted a complex railway system that had features found on real railways – cattle-

The two Märklin accessories were made c. 1902. The goods siding for loading freight, complete with signal and lamp, was available in gauges I and O. The railway restaurant kiosk was intended to be placed on the platforms of Märklin's larger railway stations.

Bing Storkleg, 1900 (F)
This is an early example of a basic, German outline Storkleg in gauge II. The presence of a coupler between the engine and the tender indicates that it was manufactured before 1902. The continental outline locomotives were almost always supplied with an unpainted, gun-metal finish, and with the steam dome and fittings in polished brass. *Sotheby's, London*

LEFT Märklin "Dutch" station, 1907 (K); Märklin glass-roofed station hall, 1904 (K); Märklin 0–4–0 electric drive, 1909 (I); Märklin 8-wheeled express coaches, 1909 (each coach G)

The gauge O 0–4–0 had a long production life and, despite its antique appearance, was still appearing in Märklin catalogues of the 1920s. The 8-wheeled express corridor coaches were another long-lived Märklin design, which was continued, with minor detail changes, for the best part of 20 years. The "Dutch" station is an example of Märklin's traditional construction methods. The unembossed, elaborately decorated walls were more typical of the Märklin style of c. 1900 than of 1907. However, this station continued to be made well into the 1920s, although the decoration was updated and applied by cheaper methods. The real gem of this scheme is the rare and elegant glass-roofed hall, which is avidly sought by collectors because the glass roof permits overhead lighting and provides a glamorous frame for the trains standing underneath.

ABOVE Märklin station, 1904 (H); Märklin French Metro, 1908 (M)

Despite the French advertisements, the Märklin passenger shelter was originally designed as the "down" side of an English station, as indicated by the high platforms. (The "up" side would have been a larger station, and a passenger footbridge over the tracks would have connected the two sides.) Pulling into the station is the evocative gauge I Märklin French Metro set. Just before World War I, Märklin designed special electric trains and underground metro sets for the United States, England and France, based on recognizable prototypes. The introduction of the German trams was delayed until after the war.

ABOVE Märklin Storkleg, 1901 (I) Märklin beer wagon, 1901 (F); Märklin open wagon with *Bremserhaus*, 1904 (D); Märklin baggage wagon with *Bremserhaus*, 1904 (C); Märklin cistern wagon with *Bremserhaus*, 1908 (F); Märklin sheep wagon, 1901 (D)
Bremserhaus is the German word for the little hut attached to a wagon in which the train guard rides; there does not seem to be an equivalent word in English. Wagons are generally more valuable if they have a *Bremserhaus* attached. The gauge I Märklin train set is fairly typical of an early period freight set; most of the wagons have iron

wheels, and some couplings are of the pre-1902 type. The locomotive is slightly earlier than the tender, the sheep wagon needs a roof and the tap handle is missing from the cistern wagon, but it is normal for the baggage wagon to have no doors. *Phillips*

BELOW Märklin 0-4-0, 1901 (F); Märklin pair of coaches, 1901 (each coach D); Märklin baggage wagon, 1901 (B); Märklin open wagon, 1902 (B)
This is basically a standard Märklin passenger set with the addition of an open freight wagon. All the couplings on the passenger set are the pre-1902

type. The general condition is quite good, although the locomotive has lost one front buffer. The absence of buffers on the passenger coaches and baggage wagon is normal for such an early set, and all early baggage wagons are without doors. The locomotive is the *de luxe* 0-4-0, with a reversing mechanism activated by the rather ugly lever running along the top of the boiler. The "skating" connecting rods allow the wheels to turn independently of one another, which is necessary because the reversing mechanism changes the wheelbase. *Phillips*

loading pens, ticket machines, telegraphs, gas lamps and bells. Differences in scale and toy-like proportions did not disturb the Germans at all, in fact they enjoyed the toy-like qualities, and Märklin, needless to say, was a great favourite.

Both Märklin and R. & G.N. (Rock & Graner, now under new management) produced complete systems of pneumatically-operated accessories, which were beautifully made and operated by compressed air in complete silence and with realistic slow motion. Issmayer made a large number of novelty automatic operating systems, which it supplied to other manufacturers; one set had a train that went into a station, automatically reversed, climbed a hill, reversed again and returned to the station. Another set featured an automatic train ferry. Of all the imaginative items produced, Märklin's track railway systems were especially elaborate, and could be bought with mountains, viaducts, elevated stations and subways. But despite its success, Märklin was finding that its traditional methods of manufacture were inadequate for supplying the low-price, mass market and, gradually, lithographed and tin-tabbed locomotives, coaches and wagons began to be added to the Märklin line to make it more competitive.

Carette and Bing had made great progress between 1900 and 1910, and their products dominated the lower end of the German market by the end of the decade. To challenge Märklin, in the luxury market, Bing kept its gauge III and IV trains in production. They were continually improved until their quality equalled those produced by Märklin. But Bing never matched the great variety nor the range of accessories that remained Märklin's great strength.

Märklin static lift bridge, 1909 (M);
Märklin island platform, 1909 (G);
Märklin central station, 1909 (M);
Märklin coaling dock, 1909 (L); Märklin
gantry crane, 1909 (I)
This extremely desirable group of Märklin accessories illustrates some of the vast range that was available. Although the central station is very large, three even larger ones were included in the 1909 catalogue. The lift bridge is one of seven different bridges. Märklin made a range of accessories for every aspect of toy rail travel, and almost all of them were interesting designs, executed with considerable charm and beautifully hand painted. It is no wonder that today's collector is willing to pay top prices for these pieces of railway fantasy. *Sotheby's, New York*

**Märklin hand-car or *Draisine*, 1907 (M);
Märklin glass-roofed station, 1907 (I)**
The inspection hand-car, with its elaborately clothed officials, runs on gauge I track, but it is made in a huge scale, much larger than any normally associated with gauge I. The figures are too big even for Märklin's extremely large gauge III. The hand-car with its doll crew may have been meant to appeal to girls. The small, glass-roofed station is barely big enough to cover the giant hand-car.

ELECTRIC POWER

Bing and the other Nuremberg firms may have been ahead in terms of construction and decoration, but they were not as adventurous in relation to motive power as Märklin, and the Göppingen firm established a clear lead in the development of electric motors. Bing did not begin to manufacture electric trains in any quantity until about 1908, and although Carette had produced an electric tram in 1892, its electric mechanisms remained crude and unreliable. (Some of the Carette motors relied on a wooden drum rubbing against a wheel as a primitive form of friction drive.) In contrast, Märklin had a full line of electric-drive steam outline locomotives as early as 1902, as well as some electric trams.

Electricity did not appeal to everyone, and the British in particular were suspicious of it. Although Bassett-Lowke and Gamage's between them listed over 300 different locomotives in 1906, only one of them, a Märklin 2-4-0 *Charles Dickens*, was electrically powered; one Carette tram was the only other electrically powered item listed for the British market.

In the United States electrically powered toy trains were not widely available until *c*.1910, when Bing and Ives added electric drive to their

Märklin round-house, 1902 (E); Märklin turntable, 1902 (B); Märklin crane, 1902 (F); Märklin snow-plough, 1902 (H)
Märklin round-houses are a problem. They are usually in very good condition, beautifully painted and large – so large and awkward, in fact, that it is difficult to know what to do with them. In consequence they are comparatively cheap. The turntable is even larger, and hardly anybody wants one. On the other hand, snow-ploughs and cranes are popular, and these two gauge II specimens are in very good condition. The crane appears to have lost its hook, but the snow-plough has its original lamp, which is very rare. To complete the snow-plough, a small crew of plaster officials and inspectors should be standing inside ready to inspect the track. *Sotheby's, New York*

Märklin *Kaiser* coach, 1901 (J); Märklin postal baggage, 1901 (I)
These gauge I coaches are among the earliest types of 8-wheeled coach made by Märklin. The word "Kaiser" refers to the crown that appears on the sides of most coaches of this type. The early painting is quite refined, and the painted curtains would be worthy of a miniaturist. Although the coach and its accompanying baggage-postal car are contemporaries, it is interesting to note the variations in the door handles and placement of the bogies. Both the roofs have been over-painted, but, fortunately, in this case, the over-painting was in water colour, which was subsequently washed off. *Phillips*

**Märklin gauge I Atlantic CEM1021, 1909
(L); Märklin postal baggage, 1902 (I);
Märklin bridge, 1902 (I)**
During the Edwardian period
(1901-10), Märklin's gauge I catalogues
could be sued to plan toy railways of
endless fantasy. Typical of the heavier
Märklin locomotives is this imaginative
recreation of a Maffei locomotive with a
wind-splitting cab, which is pulling a
train of heavy Märklin coaches, with
complete interiors and opening roofs,
over a simple, but satisfyingly realizes,
toy bridge. The bridge may be
lengthened by the addition of extra
centre piers and spans. *P. Carlson Collection*

Bing gauge IV wagons, 1904 (F), Bing gauge IV passenger brake, 1904 (J); Märklin gauge III E 3 locomotive, 1904 (M)

Bing gauge IV and Märklin gauge III both indicate the same measurement – namely 75mm between the rails – and therefore all the equipment illustrated here would run together, although it appears that one of the open wagons has lost a pair of wheels. Märklin gauge III locomotives are extremely rare, which is not surprising, since their huge boilers, tiny wheels and ungainly proportions must have discouraged buyers who preferred the sleeker products made by Bing and Carette.

Christie's, London

lines, and the products of the American firm of Lionel began to reach the customers in some quantity. Carlisle & Finch, Voltamp and the rest of the "gauge II aristocracy" had offered electric trains since 1900, but their production was small, and the effect on the toy train market was negligible.

THE RISE OF LIONEL

Of all the international toy train manufacturers in business between 1900 and 1910, the American firm of Lionel was the great maverick. Founded in 1901 by Joshua Lionel Cowan, the firm first produced $2\frac{7}{8}$in gauge, electrically-powered but clumsy tunnel locomotives and trams. To the Germans it must have appeared a typically doomed American enterprise and not to be taken seriously. But while Ives and the German manufacturers were locked in competition for the American market, Lionel was making quiet progress.

Cowan had made some shrewd observations of the American scene, and noted that most American toy train purchasers were not enthusiasts like the British, and that scale likeness and correct livery did not impress them. The typical American buyer was a fond father who wanted a good-value gift for his 12-year-old son. The complexity of a typical German toy railway seemed a needless extravagance, and accessories could always be improvised from shoe boxes and tin cans. The qualities that did impress Americans were size, price and technological innovation. Realizing that the $2\frac{7}{8}$in gauge was a hopeless commercial venture, Cowan introduced in

1906 a $2\frac{1}{8}$ in gauge, which was non-standard. Whether this was deliberate, or just an unsuccessful attempt to make a true gauge II, no one knows. But in a brilliant flash of inspiration, Cowan christened his non-standard, orphan gauge "Standard gauge". All other gauges by other manufacturers, from then on, would be "non-standard" by definition – it was a breathtaking bit of gall but it worked.

Lionel's products for the new Standard gauge were large, heavy, but simply made, locomotives, trams and rolling stock. The sectional tinplate track was based on Märklin's track, with a centre rail for electric pick-up. All the motive power was electric, and the heavy, sheet-metal construction with its thick enamel finish gave a feeling of quality. However, their simple construction meant that the trains were cheap to produce and that the price was competitive. They were the cheapest electric trains on sale – indeed, outside of a few large cities, they were the only electric trains on sale. A couple of steam outline locomotives and a variety of nicely proportioned trams were added to the line during the next four years.

Cowan had noticed that Ives had been able to compete against superior German trains with the help of a unique catalogue. Unlike other, business-oriented catalogues, which were aimed primarily at the wholesaler or toy shop, the Ives catalogue, which appeared in 1909, was written for a 12-year-old boy, was widely distributed and contained a lot of exciting railway atmosphere. In a personal letter from Harry Ives, the reader was addressed as "Division Manager" for the Ives railway system. In the letter, the "Division Manager" was cautioned that the success of the Ives miniature railway system "depends upon you as manager". This was heavy stuff for 12-year-olds, especially as parents were referred to as the "advisory board". Although this might seem pretty simple today, it was merchandizing magic in 1909, building a company loyalty that defended Ives against the German invasion as well as the challenge of the cheaper American Flyer trains – a loyalty that survived the demise of Ives, and continues up until today. In the following decade Lionel was to develop catalogues that improved upon and surpassed the Ives efforts.

4

GERMAN WORLD DOMINATION – AND ECLIPSE 1910–20

The year 1910 saw the end of a period of major developments in the toy train world. Several companies had folded – Schönner *c.*1906, Rock & Graner *c.*1904, Howard in 1910 and Beggs, which, in association with Garlick, had made only steam trains, in 1906 – unable to find the formula for success. Other firms, such as Plank and Issmayer, had lost their earlier drive and seemed to be "marking time". In America some of the recently established companies like American Flyer and Lionel were growing

Märklin L.N.W.R. *George V*, 1912 (I) ; **Bing G.N.R. Atlantic**, 1913 (H); **Bing 4-4-4**, 1913 (I); **Märklin P.L.M. Pacific**, 1914 (L)

The period just before World War I was a time of intense activity by the German manufacturers. Märklin's gauge O *George V* was an attempt to provide a steam-operated scale model for Gamage's. The single steam cylinder was inside the frame, and it drove the locomotive through gears. As an experiment, it seems to have failed for there are very few survivors. The Märklin Atlantic, on the other hand, was a more successful model and was continued for years. The steam-operated 4-4-4 was Bing's most ambitious locomotive in gauge O and is extremely rare today. Märklin's P.L.M. Pacific was made in electric, steam and clockwork and in both gauge I and gauge O. At the time, it was the company's most expensive steam outline locomotive and was carried in the catalogue for several years. Although the P.L.M. Pacific is not at all rare, it is as popular as ever, and good examples are sought after. *Courtesy London Toy and Model Museum; B. Ehrlich Collection*

stronger by providing efficiently made toys at competitive prices. In Britain, retailers such as Bassett-Lowke and Gamage's set the pace and provided a very British image for the German toy train industry. Electricity and mass production, developed in the years before 1910, were the keys to survival in the next decade.

The two German giants Märklin and Bing still considered Ives as their only real competitor in the American market; all three copied one another's products while ignoring the progress that Lionel was making, thus enabling the New York firm to gather momentum quietly. Märklin, which in the previous decade had decided to depend less on the traditional, heavy, hand-painted products, with their soldered construction, had turned to the mass-production methods of Nuremberg, using lithography and tabbed construction, even though this meant a reduction in the variety of trains on offer. With a range produced by the new methods, Märklin prepared to compete with Ives and Bing in the United

Bing 4-4-2 Atlantic, 1912 (H)

The large Bing locomotives, with their dashing wind-splitter cabs and streamlined chimneys, were very popular and were still in production well into the 1920s. They are much lighter in construction and not as well finished as Bing's British series, but their elegant good looks have ensured their appeal to today's collector. This particular gauge I engine is in a very fine, original condition, which is rare because the thin tin construction was easily dented. *Christie's, London*

Karl Bub, American train set, 1912 (F)

The products of Karl Bub, a prominent Nuremberg manufacturer, were always aimed at the lower end of the market, and they therefore tend to be rather unexciting. This handsome and well-proportioned gauge 4-4-0 is an exception, however, although the 4-wheeled coaches are very modest. The bell, cowcatcher, crosshead guide, 6-wheeled tender and long-wheelbase, leading bogie are all interesting, and they are unusual features to be found on a Bub locomotive. The box, as usual, has an exciting example of naïve railway art on the top, which promises more than it delivers. *Sotheby's, New York*

States in gauges O and I. The new lithographic process that Märklin used was superior to any other in terms of colour, lustre and detail. Beautiful green New York Central Line and red Pennsylvania Railroad coaches were brought out in 8- and 4-wheeled versions, setting new standards of realism. An extensive line of lithographed freight cars was planned and partially executed. To replace Märklin's own laboriously hand-painted engines, graceful locomotives of modern design in 0-4-0 and 4-4-0 configurations were designed to be made from lithographed parts and, for the top of the line, a stunning American 4-6-2 Pacific was produced.

Märklin also experimented with cast-iron bodies for 0-4-0s and 4-4-0s in both gauges O and I, but information about their development is scarce, and it is not known if these were dropped in favour of the lithographed locomotives or were intended to replace them. Only a handful of Märklin's cast-iron locomotives is known to exist. Special American accessories were listed, including some beautiful and elaborate stations still produced in Märklin's traditional way, which suggests that the firm regarded the locomotives and rolling stock as its first priority.

During this period, Märklin also made electric outline locomotives, good replicas of the New York Central Line's popular "S-type", in 4- and 8-wheeled versions. The 8-wheeled locomotives exist only as hand-

painted examples in gauge I, for Märklin frequently tested the market by producing a few hand-painted examples before translating the design into lithography. Unfortunately, the 8-wheeled electric locomotives were not ready in 1914, when Märklin was poised for its tremendous effort to dominate the American market. World War I intervened and put a definite end to both Märklin's expansionist plans and the beautiful new New York Central "S-class" electric.

GAUGE I FOR IVES AND BING

By 1910 Ives had added electric-drive locomotives to its line and had begun to sell the first of what was to be an impressive series of heavy, cast-iron locomotives, which featured a lot of rivet detail and were patterned after the New York Central's "S-class" electrics. These fine locomotives, particularly the 8-wheeled versions in gauge I, were Ives's leaders, and they caused quite a stir in 1910 and 1911. In 1912 Ives added to its gauge I range the most characteristic and charismatic of all the American passenger coaches, the *Observation*, with its unique and decorative open-end platform. (Surprisingly, this coach type was not added to the company's gauge O line until 1923.)

Bing lost no time in entering the American market with its own cast-iron electric outline locomotives. Its gauge I 8-wheeled electric was a close copy of the Ives locomotive, but Bing had improved upon the

Ives 3240 electric, 1912 (I)

For the electrification of its gauge I lines, Ives produced a magnificent cast-iron locomotive, patterned after the first large American electric locomotive, the 2-4-2 New York S1 class of 1906. Ives's success did not go unnoticed by Bing and Märklin. Bing produced a similar cast-iron locomotive that improved on the Ives design by placing the journal boxes more logically over the axle ends. Märklin rushed 4-wheeled versions into production and planned a super 8-wheeled electric. Lionel's large, crude, sheet steel S1 had beaten Ives by almost a year, but, as a model, it could not compare with Ives's sophistication. For some unexplained reason, Ives added another, almost identical electric to its gauge I line in 1913. The 3239 was almost a duplicate of the 3240 in construction and design but was ¾in (20mm) shorter. In 1917, both Ives locomotives were improved when the axle boxes were brought into line with the axles ends. *Torrey Collection*

American firm's design, particularly in the casting of the under-frame. Unfortunately, as had happened with Märklin, the Bing 8-wheeler was not ready in time to be listed in its 1914 catalogue.

In 1910–12 Lionel produced the first of its own sheet-metal interpretations of the ubiquitous New York Central Line's "S-class", in 4-, 6- and 8-wheeled versions. Compared with Ives products, the Lionel locomotives were big and crude, but impressive.

Lionel's success may in part be explained by its price structure compared with that of its major competitors between 1912 and 1914. In 1912, a gauge I Ives train set with a steam outline, clockwork driven 4-4-0 and three 8-wheeled passenger coaches made a train that was 4ft (1m 22cm) long and cost $17.00. A similar gauge I Bing set with two coaches, as advertised in the Sears & Roebuck catalogue, was priced at $8.95 for a train that was advertised as being 4ft (1m 22cm) long but that was in fact no longer than 3ft 10in (1m 17cm). Perhaps no one bothered to measure such things in 1912!

In contrast to these two clockwork sets, Lionel, in 1914, offered a set with an electric outline 0-4-0 and two 8-wheeled coaches, making up a train with a total length of 2ft 10½in (88cm) for only $10.00, and it was an electric-powered train. For $19.00, Lionel offered a 3-coach train which was an impressive 4ft 7in (1m 40cm) long. To most buyers, Lionel looked like the best value – well worth the small extra cost.

To offset the rather stark look of its trains, Lionel painted them with an especially thick and lustrous enamel, decorated with rubber-stamped lettering and bits of bright brass trim. The enamel finish was not as tough as lithography, nor as detailed, but, in the box at least, it had a richer look, while a painted finish allowed Lionel to offer a wider range of colours. By using cheap and effective rubber-stamped decoration, Lionel also avoided the large capital outlay required for lithographic equip-

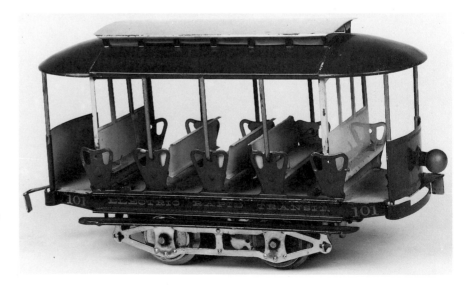

Lionel summer trolley, 1910 (L)
Lionel's trams and trolleys for its 2⅛in Standard gauge are always a favourite with collectors. Although the construction is simple, it is very strong and the proportions are charming. The play qualities of this trolley are enhanced by its open design, which meant that ''passengers'' could be easily seated and taken for a ride. The elegant lettering of the words ''electric rapid transit'' complements the nostalgic design. *Sotheby's, New York*

ment. The $2\frac{1}{8}$ in track size meant that, for the same length, Lionel trains were wider, taller and looked "heftier" than anything offered in gauge I by Bing, Märklin or Ives.

In 1912, however, Lionel was just a "small, dark cloud" on the horizon. Bing was enjoying considerable sales success, and its trains were being sold through the vast Sears & Roebuck mail order organization. Märklin was in the throes of preparing a truly superior American toy train system that would beat any competition. The German firms must have felt confident that their new train sets and aggressive pricing would prevail against Ives or any of the other American manufacturers.

World War I was to change everything. Kept out of the American market for four or five years, the Germans returned to find the rules changed. Lionel now challenged both American Flyer and Ives with its line of well-made gauge O electric trains, which had first appeared in 1915. Gauge I had been defeated by Lionel's more impressive Standard gauge, and Lionel had managed to convince the toy train buying public that lithography was a cheap and inferior process and that "wind-ups" – clockwork mechanisms – were cheap and nasty power units, which were suitable only for very small children or families too poor to afford electricity.

The Germans were appalled by this state of affairs. Moreover, American toy manufacturers had succeeded in persuading the post-war government that the toy industry in the United States was "new" and that it should, therefore, be protected from foreign competition by high protectionist tariff barriers. Märklin abandoned its projected American programme and cut its losses, off-loading its American lines on the continental market – with little success, however, for repainted American gauge I box cars were still in stock at Märklin even after World War II. Märklin had also abandoned its plan to produce for the American market a series of lithographed freight cars, which would have closely resembled the Ives and Bing cars. Little is known of this series, which was never catalogued, but it is believed that it included as many as 17 different cars, all 8-wheelers. Occasionally, when one of the cars appears for sale, it is usually identified as a Bing item, even though Märklin's shield trademark is incorporated into the lithography.

Bing, better established and better known, continued to struggle, even though the mighty Sears & Roebuck organization switched to American Flyer products for its 1919 catalogue, and the great Bing gauge O series of lithographed freight stock had been superseded by a similar Ives line. Lionel's large, reasonably priced electric trains had killed the American market for quality clockwork, and gauge I had been eclipsed by Standard gauge. The profits on cheap clockwork trains became very marginal because of the high tariffs on imports and the increased shipping costs from Europe. Steam outline locomotives began to look old-fashioned and they were replaced by the new electric outline trains, which were what the customers wanted, as the increasing sales of the Lionel electrics indicated. Bing's best chance for competing in the

American market lay in producing small gauge O electric-drive locomotives. The future for the German firm looked black, but, with new financing, Bing kept a hold on the market, even though Prohibition in 1919 meant that the word "beer" had to be painted out by hand on every Bing beer refrigerator car.

GERMAN MONOPOLY OF BRITISH MARKETS

In Britain in 1910 the Germans were in complete control of the toy train market, and the few British manufacturers of brass "dribblers" were completely outclassed. The aims of the German toy train industries, by this time, had become much more refined. Large, expensive, gauge I locomotives made by Bing and Märklin were sold exclusively through Gamage's and Bassett-Lowke. Cheaper sets made by Bing, Carette, Karl Bub, Kraus, Fischer and others were sold through high street toy shops and the large department stores. The huge variety that had flooded the

British market between 1900 and 1910 had been replaced by more logical and limited ranges.

Märklin offered a fine series of mass-produced, lithographed passenger coaches, freight stock and even a few lithographed locomotives in gauges O and I, while the firm's gauge II and III ranges for the English market were completely withdrawn from sale. Märklin's new lithographed passenger coaches were similar to the 1909 Carette range, but the Märklin lithographic painting gave richer colours, and the coaches, which were distributed through Gamage's, reached a wider market.

By 1910, Carette had realized that Bassett-Lowke was not going to be the mass outlet it had hoped for, and by 1914 the firm offered a new line of improved passenger coaches, with interiors and opening doors. The coaches carried Carette's own trademark, and they were intended to be sold through a wide range of toy retailers, rather than exclusively through Bassett-Lowke. Carette's fine range of semi-scale lithographed freight stock was also re-designed for mass distribution. The extremely pretty, well-proportioned and lithographed Carette scale locomotives had been sold exclusively through Bassett-Lowke. The range had, however, been unsuccessful, partly because of the very light construction, which made them seem flimsy, and partly because of the cheap and inadequate mechanisms, which wore out quickly. Carette dropped these locomotives from its line and was in the process of introducing a new line of more toy-like and robust locomotives in 1914. The production of this interesting new line was stopped by World War I. Georges Carette, who had retained his French citizenship, had to return to his native country when war broke out, and his factory in Nuremberg closed down in 1917, never to reopen. A small number of "Carette" locomotives and other toys continued to be produced after the war by Fleischmann, Bassett-Lowke and others, using some of the old Carette tooling.

BELOW Bing for Bassett-Lowke G.N.R. Atlantic, 1912 (I); Carette for Bassett-Lowke G.N.R. *Clemenson* **coach, 1910 (D)**
The gauge I Bing Atlantic was one of the largest locomotives in Bing's British locomotive range and one of the earliest. It was a very popular locomotive and was made over a long period of time in steam, electric and clockwork and in two different gauges, O and I. The electric version, shown here, has a movable flap between the splashers, which allows the gears to be oiled. The *Clemenson* coach, so called because of the compensating 6-wheeled system used, is quite rare in Great Northern Railway colours and was usually sold in sets of three. *Sotheby's, London*

FAR BELOW Carette for Bassett-Lowke M.R. coach, 1910 (E); Carette for Bassett-Lowke G.W.R. coach, 1910 (E)
To accompany Bing's series of special British locomotives, Carette produced a selection of finely lithographed coaches that reached new heights of scale accuracy. The lithography was extremely accurate, and today these gauge I coaches could be used as guides for finishing scale models. Although these two clerestory coaches are the same size and have similar roofs, Carette went to the extra effort to reproduce the characteristic M.R. windows and roof ventilation. *Sotheby's, London*

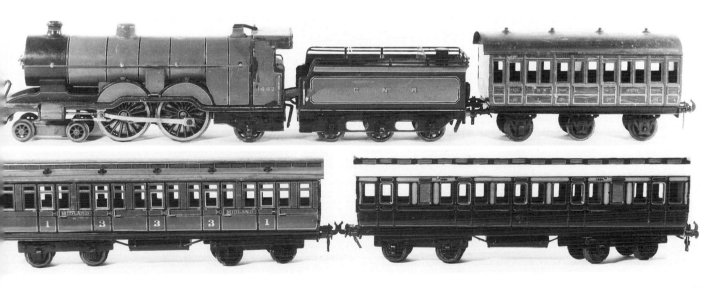

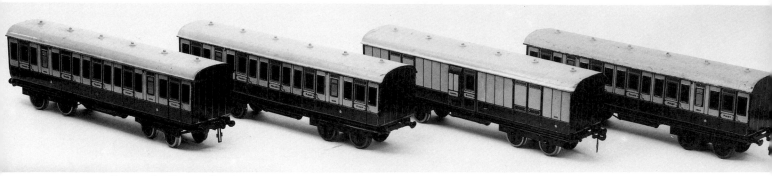

ABOVE Carette for Bassett-Lowke L.N.W.R. passenger coaches, 1910 (each coach D)

The Carette range of lithographed coaches for Bassett-Lowke was the most ambitious series of passenger coaches ever produced by any toy train manufacturer before World War I. The beautiful and accurate lithography was manufactured from designs supplied by Henry Greenly, the noted British miniature train expert. In order to save weight and allow long trains to be pulled, no interiors were included, and the construction was light and strong. Six railway companies were catered for. Great Northern, London & North-Western, London and South Western, North Eastern, Midland and Great Western. The number of different designs spread over gauges O, I, II and III amounted to a grand total of 62, including such special coaches as the L.N.W.R. 12-wheeled dining saloon, the 6-wheeled *Clemensons* and the travelling post offices. *Phillips*

ABOVE RIGHT Carette Storkleg, 1912 (E)

Carette was one of the last of the German manufacturers to persist with the outdated Storkleg design, and the gauge I example illustrated is the final design. The lithographed cab and tender, stamped tin wheels and oscillating cylinders show that Carette was becoming adept at producing steam locomotives at a competitive price. The styling is rather nondescript, but the American-styled cab is an indication of Carette's export thinking. *Sotheby's, London*

ABOVE Carette for Bassett-Lowke *Peckett* tank, 1910 (G)

"Peckett" was the name of the manufacturer of the prototype for this popular industrial locomotive. Although the proportions are far too large for true scale O, the appeal of this little locomotive was undeniable, and the manufacture of this design was continued by Bassett-Lowke long after Carette's demise. Versions were made in gauges O, I and II, but the motive power was always clockwork. *Phillips*

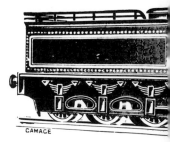

In 1914 Bing was attempting to upgrade its antiquated stock, which had begun to suffer in comparison with Märklin and Carette. Bing had ambitious plans for a new line of lithographed coaches and freight wagons, but none of the new items was delivered before the war, and the company had to wait until 1919 before shipments could be made. These new Bing lithographed coaches were the most elaborate yet produced. They had working doors and full interiors, and they set a standard for British outline rolling stock that was never equalled by any other toy maker. The gauge I coaches were so large that they could have been used for gauge II. Bing locomotives for the British market were regularly upgraded, and new items came on to the market every year. The scale series for Bassett-Lowke, which had been started in 1904, received new additions regularly in gauges O, I, II and III, and, in the period just before the war, met the very highest standards of design and finish. The series of locomotives that Bing made for Bassett-Lowke was one of the finest series ever produced, and existing examples are usually in excellent condition, for they have been treasured over the years by their owners.

Bing made locomotives for both Bassett-Lowke and Gamage's. The cheaper locomotives had a tabbed construction and were finished with

ABOVE Two of Märklin's simple but well finished lithographed coaches, dating from c.1913. They were available in the liveries of the London & North Western, the Midland and the Great Northern Railways and in gauges I and O.

LEFT The imposing London & North Western Railway 4–6–0 *Experiment*, which was made c.1913 by Märklin in both gauges O and I, but only in clockwork.

lithographic printing; the more expensive ones were soldered and hand painted. The entire range set new standards of quality and design. For Bassett-Lowke Bing concentrated mainly on items in gauge I, with gauge O second in popularity. However, Bing also added to the gauge II and III range occasionally, and Bassett-Lowke's 1914 catalogue lists 39 gauge I locomotives, 28 gauge O, 12 gauge II and 2 gauge III, giving a total of 81 different locomotives. Clockwork and steam were still the most popular sources of power, and only 16 of the 81 had electric motors. Trams, trolleys and electric outline locomotives had all disappeared from the Bassett-Lowke range by 1914; only steam outline locomotives remained.

Märklin introduced British outline locomotives made in the new "Nuremberg style" to compete with Bing and Carette across the entire price range. At the lower end of the market were inexpensive, but well-made, lithographed 0-4-0s and 4-wheeled passenger coaches in gauges O and I. At the market's upper end were hand-finished, large 6-coupled locomotives in both gauges, available in clockwork, electric or steam. Märklin had wanted the large engines to be scale models, and they were almost as good as Bing's locomotives – however, they were larger and cheaper. Most of Märklin's hand-painted rolling stock had been dropped by 1914 to make the trimmed-down Märklin range ready for competition. There had been a few setbacks, and some of Märklin's most ambitious series of locomotives had been failures.

In 1910 Bassett-Lowke had again considered Märklin as a supplier of scale models, and the German firm had responded by designing a very good scale outline L.N.W.R. 4-4-2T *Precursor* tank locomotive in gauge I. The locomotive was steam powered and driven by a single, concealed cylinder, geared to the driving wheels. It could be made to go in reverse by changing the gears, just like a clockwork locomotive. Companion locomotives were made with clockwork and electric drive. Bassett-Lowke included these locomotives briefly around 1910 but then quickly dropped them, probably because the steam locomotive gave insufficient power. Whatever the reason, another 25 years went by before Bassett-Lowke again considered Märklin as a supplier.

This rejection by Bassett-Lowke did not dampen Märklin's enthusiasm for its new steam designs, and two revamped locomotives

LEFT Märklin L.N.W.R. Bowen-Cooke, 1914 (L)
The locomotives Märklin produced for Gamage's were, in general, larger and heavier than their rivals made by Bing for Bassett-Lowke. The Märklin locomotives, such as this gauge I tank engine, which is named *Bowen-Cooke* after its designer, have interesting but exaggerated detailing, such as the round wash-out plugs on the boiler and the door handle of the smoke-box. The paint finish is good and has the typical Märklin painted rivets, but it is not up to the Bing standard, and over the years examples tend to suffer from crazing caused by the varnish shrinking. This example is free from the crazing, but someone has knocked the cab roof forward. *Sotheby's, London*

RIGHT Bing L.N.W.R. 0-4-0 steamer, 1912 (H)
Bing locomotives for the British market were frequently the best available, and this neatly designed gauge I steamer is no exception. The workmanship is solid and well designed, and the finish is superb. The steamer is equipped with valve gear, reversing block, whistle and double-acting, fixed cylinders, and it has a piston oiler, which is accessible through the working smoke-box door. One drawback was the externally fired boiler, which made it very likely that the paint finish on the boiler would be burned off with use. *Sotheby's, London*

BELOW RIGHT Bing for Bassett-Lowke 6-coupled tank, 1912 (I)
Bing's large and impressive 6-coupled tank engines were made in gauge II only. A gauge I user had to be content with Märklin's *Bowen-Cooke*, which was similar (see above). As a companion for the London & North-Western Railway locomotive, Bing made a similar engine for the Great Central. The clockwork mechanisms for these Bing 6-coupled locomotives were very powerful, and they had enormous springs to ensure long runs. Electric versions were also available. *Sotheby's, London*

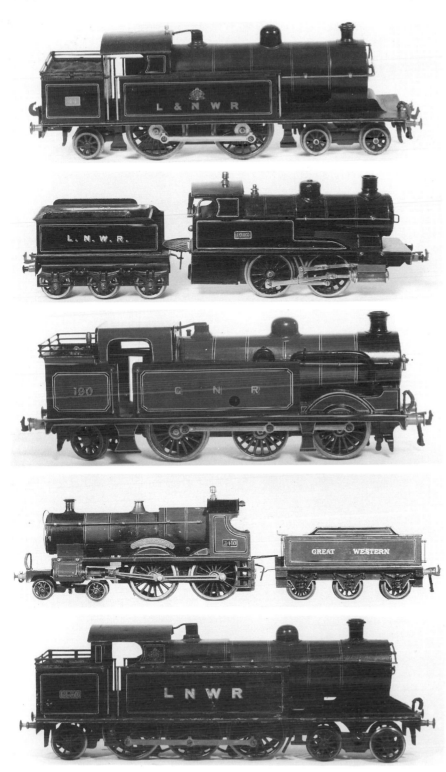

Bing for Bassett-Lowke L.N.W.R. *Precursor* tank, 1912 (G)

This popular gauge I locomotive got its nickname *Precursor* tank because it was a tender-less development of the famous London & North-Western Railway 4-4-0 *Precursor* (see page 66). Because Bing also made a *Precursor* for Bassett-Lowke, the two different locomotives are frequently confused. The *Precursor* tank was the most popular of Bing's classic range of British locomotives, and good examples are relatively easy to find. Märklin also made a similar locomotive, and, although rarer than the Bing model, it is in the same price range, probably because its slightly coarser proportions have less appeal. *Sotheby's, London*

Bing for Bassett-Lowke, G.N.R. condensing tank, 1912 (I)

Bing's gauge II Great Northern Railway tank engine is quite a good model of the prototype of a class of tank engines specially designed for running in underground tunnels. The condensing apparatus was an effort to reduce smoke and fumes. The large pipes necessary for its operation give the locomotive the distinctive appearance that made it popular, and relatively large numbers were sold. *Sotheby's, London*

Bing for Bassett-Lowke G.W.R. *County of Northampton*, 1910 (J)

In its classic range for Bassett-Lowke, Bing did not include very many Great Western locomotives. However, this 4-4-0 "County" class was available as a steamer in gauges I, II and III. The nameplate is a bit of a joke because there is no county named "Northampton"; the name actually commemorates the site of Bassett-Lowke's head office. Usually, most of the paint is burnt off the boiler of Bing steamers, but this gauge I example is in exceptionally good condition, with almost all of the paint intact. *Christie's, London*

Märklin L.N.W.R. *Bowen-Cooke,* 1913 (L); **Carette M.R.** *Peckett,* 1910 (G); **Bing for Bassett-Lowke S.E.C.R.** *Wainwright,* 1914 (L); **Bing for Bassett-Lowke C.R.** *Dunalastair,* 1914 (L) The period just before World War I was the heyday of gauge I, particularly of British outline locomotives. With guidance from Bassett-Lowke and Gamage's, German manufacturers produced a very large range of realistic, beautifully finished locomotives with good proportions. Because they were expensive for their time, they were well looked after, and survivors are usually in good condition. The Caledonian Railway *Dunalastair* was found in almost mint condition in a Dutch flea market. *Courtesy London Toy and Model Museum; P. Carlson Collection*

appeared in the 1912 Gamage's catalogue. Both were steam-driven L.N.W.R. 4-4-0 *George V* tender locomotives in gauges I and O. The gauge I locomotive had two concealed steam cylinders and a gear drive with a gear reverse; the gauge O locomotive had a single, concealed, steam cylinder and geared drive, but a slip-eccentric reversing mechanism. They were in Gamage's 1912 and 1913 catalogues, but, although significant design changes were introduced for 1914, the locomotives were still troublesome and were dropped. Five examples of the gauge O locomotive still exist, making it one of the rarest and least known of all Märklin locomotives, yet one of the most interesting technically.

The war had as disastrous an effect on the English companies as on their German suppliers. Although posing as a British manufacturer, Bassett-Lowke in fact imported almost all its ready-to-run railway items from Germany. The 1916 catalogue included the following statement:

> Owing to the War and the impossibility of obtaining mechanical toys from abroad, many of our lower-priced locomotives have had to be cancelled. The same applies to several of our well-known models where we have been dependent upon the Continent for clockwork movements, piston valve cylinders and permanent magnet motors. We are distinctly an all-British firm, English capital, English directors, English staff and over 80% of the articles sold by us are British, made throughout in our works at Northampton.

There was no mention at all of Germany in this misleading bluster, which equated a British-made brass screw with a Bing gauge I locomotive.

FRENCH TRAINS FROM MÄRKLIN

In France, Märklin had no real competition for the luxury market, although the large Bing trains in gauges III and IV were great favourites with the French. No French manufacturers could supply anything as good as Märklin's new P.L.M. 4-6-2 Pacific, which was available in gauges I or O. This locomotive, which first appeared in 1912, was the high point of the firm's pre-war production. Large and handsome with intriguing detail, it was offered in steam, clockwork and electric, and it was a resounding sales success, even though the long P.L.M. coaches designed to accompany it did not appear until after the war. Although its sales success meant that it could never be considered a rare locomotive, it

Märklin for Gamage's M.R. 4-4-0, 1912 (G)
The Midland Railway 4-4-0 was a popular locomotive in spite of its awkward looks, probably because it was cheaper than the equivalent locomotive by Bing for Bassett-Lowke. Although there is extensive crazing, the paint appears to be intact on this gauge I engine, and the typical Märklin touches, such as the boiler wash-out plugs, delicate safety valve casting and hand-painted rivets, are all quite evident. The cranked winding handle, provided with many Märklin locomotives, was much easier to use than a key. *Phillips*

is still much sought after by collectors. Apart from this spectacular engine and a few P.L.M. *Coupé Vent* 4-4-0s, the French had to content themselves with English and German outline locomotives, augmented by occasional items of North American rolling stock. Even the Märklin 8-wheeled electric outline PO El for the French market was the old Central London Underground railway design, painted green and topped with an added pantograph. In Märklin's pre-war French edition catalogue only four pieces of rolling stock are specifically French, compared with 12 American designs. Bing, Carette and the other German manufacturers did not develop specifically French designs; they competed against French manufacturers with a mixture of British- and German-styled trains, much in the way they had done in the previous decade.

THE GERMAN HOME MARKET

German toy train buyers in 1910 were still obsessed with complex toy railroads, and the variety of accessories on offer in Germany was much greater than anywhere else. However, a new realism was gaining ground, and many of the old, fanciful accessories were no longer produced, or were replaced with new, simpler and, in many cases, rather dull items. The great terminus stations, magnificent tin-plate palaces, were still well represented, and no other company surpassed Märklin in this area of railway art. The traditional methods of soldering and hand painting served Märklin well in the home market, for they allowed a number of different buildings to be constructed from a combination of a few basic pressings and castings. It is interesting today to examine a group of Märklin buildings and to determine how many different parts were made by the same tool. Cheap but skilled German labour was the key to the variety, as well as the quality of the German hand-made goods.

World War I was a disaster for the German toy industry. Toy train factories were diverted into the making of munitions, and many never

Issmayer (probably) mail train set, 1912 (F)
The winged wheel trademark was occasionally used by Issmayer, but otherwise there is no maker's mark on this charming little set. Issmayer was fond of mechanical novelty, and the ingenious mail-bag pick-up device is typical of the company's cheap but effective mechanisms. The box itself has a wonderful label, full of intricate detail but with only a passing similarity to the simple 0-4-0 inside. *Phillips*

recovered from the effects of war and the economic chaos that followed. Märklin, which had worked so hard to catch up with the lead established by Bing with its mass-production methods, was especially hard hit. But if the war was a setback for Märklin, it was considerably worse for Carette, which went out of business in 1917. The new Carette lines for the German and English markets had been marketed briefly in Austria in 1914–16, and British outline Carettes may be found today in places like Vienna, although none appear in London. When Georges Carette retired to Paris in 1917 some of the firm's dies and tools were acquired by Winteringham, a British company, which took up manufacturing for Bassett-Lowke, and the tools enabled a few products of Carette origin to be included in the Bassett-Lowke catalogue as late as 1940.

The remainder of the Carette plant and tools was shared out among various German manufacturers: Karl Bub took over the automobiles and Fleischmann the boats. The highpoints of the Carette line, however, such as the incredible, lithographed scale model of the English Harrow station, the water tower with advertising signs and the S.E.C. & C. steam railcar disappeared, and the delicacy and flair of those designs were never equalled by any other manufacturer. The demise of Carette was particularly unfortunate because the company was just entering a new and confident phase, and the last Carette products had a distinct style and beauty, superior to anything that it had produced before.

During the first two years after the war, the German manufacturers enjoyed some success. They were able to deliver many shipments that had been blocked by the war; Bing's new line of lithographed locomotives and the *de luxe* scale passenger coaches, planned in 1914, reached Bassett-Lowke, for example, and Märklin stock, including the new 4-4-2 North British Atlantic, was on sale at Gamage's. But it was a short-lived boom. The great days of expensive toy railroads for enthusiasts were over, as other hobbies syphoned off available money. There was still a demand for cheap train sets, and Bing was in the best position, continuing to sell countless numbers of its cheap sets during a brief Indian summer of prominence in the British market.

The section of the market that catered for adult enthusiasts was hit hard, however. Although Märklin's long P.L.M. coaches enjoyed good sales for many years, the firm's 1919 catalogue contained many tantalizing fragments of the aborted pre-war programmes, which, after a brief appearance, were never seen again. Märklin's projected gauge III sets for the United States, France and Germany were a great loss to the toy train scene, judging from the isolated examples illustrated in the catalogue.

The German manufacturers were, however, most badly affected by the new competition that appeared after World War I from British firms such as Whitanco, Wells, Brimtoy, Chad Valley and, especially, Hornby, while the new strength of American firms like Ives, Lionel, American Flyer and Dorfan meant that the German monopoly of the toy train world had come to an end.

5
THE TOY TRAIN BOOM 1920–30

The years immediately after World War I saw the German toy industry in confusion. It was suffering from protectionist tariffs, inflation at home, increased labour costs and higher shipping costs. American, British and French toy train makers were able to take full advantage of these circumstances during the 1920s.

In the United States, Ives was no longer the company to be watched. As we have seen (pages 84–5), Lionel had seized the initiative with its non-standard Standard gauge, efficient manufacturing and progressive marketing. Refuting doubts about the realism of its trains, Lionel loudly proclaimed that, indeed, its trains were different: they were more realistic than any others. These claims were repeated in advertising and in a series of beautifully printed full-colour catalogues, which were addressed to "boys", and they were believed.

Not all of Lionel's claims were idle boasting: its trains were very strongly built and had powerful motors, and they had a confident styling that was, unmistakably, Lionel. The smaller, more refined number I gauge products from Ives and Bing definitely looked inferior to the Lionel products.

After the war, Bing had brought out its new, gauge I cast-iron, 8-wheeled electric locomotive – but too late. Ives's own 8-wheeled electrics were losing ground to Lionel products, and although Bing quickly designed new electric locomotives, made from sheet steel, with rivet detail and lots of bright brass trim, like those made by Lionel, gauge I could not compete with Lionel's larger Standard gauge. Believing that gauge O stood a better chance, Bing, in a fit of desperation, took its new sheet-metal, 12-wheeled gauge I electric, painted it Ives orange and mounted it on gauge O bogies. This locomotive, with three converted gauge I passenger coaches, made an impressive but extremely clumsy gauge O train, and it did not sell well. Bing's next attempt to regain a hold in the American market was to convert its gauge I rolling stock to Lionel's Standard gauge by mounting them on larger bodies. But the already undersized Bing cars compared poorly with the larger Lionel cars. No longer sure of its direction, no longer having a price advantage, and unable to assimilate the new style, Bing gradually disappeared from the American scene.

STANDARD GAUGE FOR THE AMERICANS
By the 1920s Lionel's Standard gauge had become the yardstick against which other toy train manufacturers were judged in America. Ives, for example, had to adopt Lionel's Standard gauge or be relegated to the status of a minor, gauge O manufacturer. In 1921, therefore, Ives

ABOVE Dayton "Hill Climber" tram, 1920 (B); Dayton "Hill Climber" 2-4-2, 1920 (C)

The sheet-steel products of the Dayton company were called "Hill Climbers" because they were powered by a friction motor containing a large iron flywheel. If the iron flywheel could be turned fast enough, they would, indeed, climb hills. Like most American floor toys, they were enormously strong and rather crude, but there is a certain pleasingly primitive quality about them and the locomotive's proportions are quite good. *Sotheby's, New York*

RIGHT Lionel 408E train set, 1927 (K)

The *de luxe* version of the 402 electric locomotive had quite a bit of added detail, including extra headlamps, handrails, piping and large working pantographs, which are unfortunately missing from this example. With two motors, the Standard gauge 408E could easily haul four of Lionel's heavy coaches, complete with 6-wheeled bogies and full interiors. These very large Lionel trains were extremely strong and, with their bright colours satisfying bulk and numerous play features, must have been one of the most thrilling toy trains ever to appear under a Christmas tree. *Sotheby's, New York*

abandoned gauge I and its connotions of European trains and adopted "Wide gauge", so called by Ives because Lionel had a copyright on the phrase "Standard gauge". The new electric locomotives and rolling stock offered by Ives followed Lionel's styling but improved upon it. The new, sleek Ives line made Lionel trains look old fashioned and crude, for Ives proportions were better, rivets abounded and everything was painted with heavy enamel, with rubber-stamped lettering and decoration; lithographic decoration was banished to the cheap gauge O sets. One lonely, cast-iron, steam outline Wide gauge 0-4-0 was kept in production to continue Ives steam train tradition.

Ives new line proved popular, but the firm was less successful in following Lionel's manufacturing methods. Piece for piece, Ives trains cost more to make, and, in any case, Lionel was already well along with plans for a brand new line that would be far ahead of anything else. The design and die work for Lionel's new range was transferred to a firm in

ABOVE Lionel 402 train set, 1925 (H)
The 402 electric locomotive was a loose
interpretation of a New York Central
"S-class", tunnel locomotive, with a
tiny pantograph, which was a feature of
the prototype. The design of this $2\frac{1}{8}$in
Standard gauge set, by the Lionel design
office in Naples, Italy, broke new
ground in toy train design. The
locomotive and coaches are very large
but constructed from relatively few
heavy steel stampings, welded and
clipped together. Assembly was simple
and could be done by unskilled labour.
Details were emphasized by brass-
coloured, clip-on parts, and they were
painted in heavy, lustrous enamel, with
rubber-stamped lettering. *Sotheby's, New York*

**ABOVE LEFT Lionel 390E 2-4-2, 1929 (F);
Lionel 300 series passenger cars, 1928
(each car B)**
For most of the 1920s, Standard gauge
steam outline locomotives were
neglected and the electrics were the
glamour engines. By the end of the
decade, Lionel had begun to reintroduce a varied line of steam outline
locomotives, constructed out of sheet-
steel pressings and pressure die-
castings. The die-castings were a new
departure for most of the toy train
firms, but almost all of them had trouble
with metal fatigue in the castings due to
contamination of the metal. It is rare to
find an early die-cast Lionel locomotive
with all its castings intact. *Sotheby's, New York*

Naples, Italy, called La Precisa, and, in 1924, the first product of the
Italian connection was on the market. It was the 402, a good looking and
strong 8-wheeled electric, based on the New York Central "S-class", but
painted an attractive Italian State Railways brown. Using the original
Lionel system of one-piece construction from heavy sheet steel, the
Italian designers created a new toy aesthetic from a few simple, basic
shapes. Nothing like it had been produced before in either Europe or
America. The traditional Lionel steam outline locomotives were
dropped, and the new Lionel line was entirely electric outline. The new
locomotives and rolling stock were larger and much stronger than those
in the previous range, more use was made of embossing, and brass trim
was lavishly used for journal boxes, window frames and other details.

With the introduction of its new trains, Lionel began to move away

**Lionel 300 "Hell Gate" bridge (H);
Lionel 381 passenger set (L); Lionel 436
power station, 1926 (D); Lionel 129
station, 1920 (C)**
The "Hell Gate" bridge was an
exceptionally clever Standard gauge
design, which did not require the train
to change elevation while crossing and
therefore eliminated the need for
approach ramps. Because it was
relatively short, it also allowed a very
large bridge to be fitted into a very
small space. The power station could be
used on its own or it could contain a
transformer. The skylight was
removable so that controls were
accessible. The lighter, 400 series
coaches were a better match for the
underpowered 381 locomotive than the
large *State* coaches originally supplied.
Sotheby's, New York

from the drab blacks, maroons and dark olive greens that were
characteristic of its early production. Now Lionel trains were painted in
brilliant blues, light greens, rich tans, primary reds and other wonderful
colours that had never been seen on full-sized American trains. They
were true toy train colours, and with this combination of size, glitter and
colour, Lionel reached the acme of American toy train production. The
381, a giant 12-wheeled bi-polar electric, pulling a train of four State
Pullmans, each $21\frac{1}{2}$in (54cm) long with full interiors, lights, brass fittings
and riding on 12 wheels, made up a train that was to remain the supreme
achievement of the American toy train industry.

Until the 1920s, American Flyer had been content to compete in the
American market with the cheap Bing and Ives cast-iron wind-ups.
However, at the opening of the new decade the firm began to show signs
of greater ambitions. In an ill-advised effort, American Flyer tried in 1925
to market cast-iron engines and lithographed coaches in Britain under
the name "British Flyer". Although the trains were specially designed in a
British style, the cast-iron engines and toy-like coaches did not meet with
much approval in the British market, and "British Flyer" died an early
death.

With more success, American Flyer entered the Standard gauge
market in 1925 with a line of large and good-looking equipment. For its
first year's production, American Flyer bought passenger coaches from
Lionel, painting and lettering them for its own trains. When American
Flyer's own passenger stock came on to the market, the sides were
effectively decorated with lithographic printing. American Flyer aimed to
compete directly with Lionel, and its trains were larger and cheaper than

comparable Lionel trains. Although the lithographed coaches were not as successful as American Flyer had hoped and were eventually replaced by coaches decorated in the Lionel style – enamel paint, brass window trim and name-plates – the large American Flyer trains gave Lionel cause for concern. Consequently, plans were made to produce train sets that would give Lionel unchallenged supremacy in Standard gauge. The giant

Lionel 381E, 1928 (J)
The largest Lionel Standard gauge electric locomotive was this 12-wheeled monster, which used a Milwaukee Road bi-polar locomotive as a prototype. Designed to haul four giant *State* coaches, the 381 was a disappointment because its single motor did not deliver enough power, and the twin-motored 402 type had to be hurriedly supplied as a substitute. A very expensive locomotive until recently, the 381 has seen its value eroded by the excellent reproduction by Williams. *Sotheby's, New York*

Lionel 402 electric, 1928 (E); Lionel 211 flat car, 1926 (B); Lionel 219 crane, 1926 (C); Lionel 215 tank car, 1925 (B); Lionel 212 gondola with containers, 1926 (E); Lionel 218 dump car, 1926 (B)
The 200 series freight cars were the largest ever to be offered by Lionel. By the mid-1920s, the Lionel style, using brass plates for most of the lettering and sporting brass journal boxes and brake wheels, was well established. Because of their immense popularity and high survival rate, Lionel Standard gauge freight cars are not at all rare and represent very good value for money. *Sotheby's, New York*

American Flyer "Pocohontas" set, 1928 (H)
The Wide gauge (2¼in), bi-polar locomotive, introduced in 1928, was a brand new addition to the American Flyer line, and the Lionel-style coaches were a generous 14in (36cm) long, complete with internal lighting. The whole train was an impressive 6ft 7in (2 metres) long, and a complete set weighed more than 30lb (13.6kg).
Sotheby's, New York

Blue Comet and *State* sets by Lionel were to surpass anything by American Flyer or by any other toy train manufacturer.

By the mid-1920s Ives had realized that radical action had to be taken if it was to survive. A substantial sum of money was borrowed and plunged into a new line to rival Lionel. Cast iron, which was heavy and too weak for the large gauge, was replaced by light and strong die-castings. A new 4-4-2 steam outline locomotive was designed that would be made largely of die-castings. The new engine was impressively large, had good proportions and was equipped with an advanced ball-bearing motor. New 21in (53cm) passenger coaches were planned to complement the new steamer and the new, bi-polar-type electrics. Manufacturing

procedures were rationalized and the new line was engineered for ease of production. It was an ambitious and well-planned effort, but Ives's finances were not strong enough to carry the programme through, and the firm went bankrupt in 1928.

However, 1928 was not the end of Ives; the firm was to continue for two more years under the joint control of Lionel and American Flyer, and for a final two years under the sole control of Lionel. From 1928 on, the Ives line became a complex jumble of Ives, American Flyer and Lionel equipment.

The year after the Ives bankruptcy, 1929 (also the year of the Wall Street Crash), saw the introduction of the greatest Ives train of all time – the magnificent, copper-plated *Prosperity Special*, pulled by a giant, die-cast, steam outline 4-4-2. It was a golden train intended to celebrate the close of a golden decade. However, the train quickly vanished, the irony of its name perhaps too harsh a reminder of the decline of American prosperity.

The financing from Lionel and American Flyer meant that the new, big die-cast Ives locomotives could be marketed, although the Ives 21in (53cm) passenger coaches never appeared. Both Lionel and American Flyer had thought that the Ives name would be a help in selling more trains. However, the venture did not work, and American Flyer was the first to get out, selling its interest to Lionel, which continued to be involved for another two years. Lionel even created brand new trains to be sold under the Ives name, but conditions were changing fast, and they were not successful. The Depression was deepening, and when Lionel abandoned the operation in 1932, Ives railways finally vanished for ever.

The three major, Standard-gauge manufacturers in the United States – Lionel, American Flyer and Ives – had two interesting rivals: Dorfan and Boucher. Dorfan was a small, but technologically advanced, company based in Newark, New Jersey. It was partially financed by the family that owned the German firm of Kraus, and there were close links with Nuremberg factories, especially Bing. Dorfan was one of the first companies to use pressure die-castings, whose precision allowed the bodies of the locomotives to double as frames for the motors. Rolling stock was attractively lithographed and set off by a liberal sprinkling of brass highlights, bright colours and well detailed die-castings.

Dorfan's chief competitive advantage lay in the superior power of its locomotives. The rather heavy rolling stock made the additional power necessary, and Dorfan locomotives of c.1926 could easily outperform anything produced by Ives, Lionel or American Flyer. Although the die-castings gave Dorfan a manufacturing edge, they proved to be the firm's Achilles' heel. Unbreakable and lightweight when new, the castings, in time, began to suffer from what the Germans called *Zinc Pest* (metal fatigue), and they expanded, cracked and warped. Dorfan trains gradually disintegrated into mounds of rubble, and only a few survive unscathed today to remind us of the firm's former glories. In addition to their tall, art deco-styled, Standard gauge locomotives, Dorfan also made

LEFT **American Flyer *President's Special*, 1928 (L)**
The Wide gauge trains of American Flyer were strong competition for Lionel's 2⅛in Standard gauge, and the top of the line was the magnificent *President's Special*, which had newly designed coaches for 1928. The 12-wheeled locomotive was made by simply adding a couple of 4-wheeled units to the basic 4-wheeled, box-cab electric. The new 19in (48cm) passenger cars were entirely in the Lionel style, with heavy steel stampings, painted in "Rolls Royce" blue, and decorated with brass trim. They replaced the innovative, but short-lived, lithographed coaches. *Sotheby's, New York*

Dorfan set, 1928 (G)
Despite close links with the European firm of Fandor/Kraus, Dorfan products had an all-American look. Technically advanced, this Standard gauge set made extensive use of die-casting. Unfortunately for Dorfan, metal fatigue has caused most of its output to turn into piles of grey dust. *Courtesy London Toy and Model Museum*

a small selection of very appealing gauge O trains in the late 1920s, but after 1929, when it became necessary to produce cheaper trains, there was a marked loss of quality, and the firm did not survive long after 1936.

The other Standard gauge manufacturer competing with Ives, Lionel and American Flyer was the well-established New York model-boat firm of Boucher, which had bought up Voltamp (see pages 47–9) in the early 1920s. Although Boucher had changed Voltamp's line to Standard gauge, in all other respects the old Voltamp trains remained unchanged until the end of the 1920s. These antique trains, with their primitive construction, were bought by a tiny handful of wealthy and conservative enthusiasts. Boucher's only new design was the *Blue Comet*, a revamped Voltamp 4-6-2 Pacific, which pulled three large, well-proportioned coaches. A small number of these very large trains was made at the end of the 1920s and early 1930s. Although the coaches were large, they were simply constructed of wood and steel and lacked interior detail. However, it was an imposing train and helped to swell the already impressive number of Standard gauge trains in production at the end of the 1920s.

While attention was focused on Standard gauge, gauge O soldiered quietly on, very much the poor relation. Trains offered for sale included Bing electrics, made from cast-iron and from sheet steel, and both Ives and American Flyer made large numbers of cheap cast-iron locomotives that were indistinguishable from one another. American Flyer produced

a *de luxe* 12-wheeled electric outline engine, but Lionel had the most ambitious range, and its large 8-wheeled electric was available with two motors. Dorfan's die-cast locomotives and lithographed rolling stock were unusually attractive, but, in the final analysis, the excitement and glamour of the 1920s toy train market in the United States was provided by Standard gauge, and the giant and colourful Standard gauge trains on sale in 1929 were to be the high-water mark of the American toy industry.

HORNBY STARTS MANUFACTURING TOY TRAINS

In the early 1920s *the* great name in British toy train manufacture, Frank Hornby's Meccano Company, started to produce British trains at its factory in Liverpool. In 1901 Hornby had obtained a patent for the Meccano construction system, which he called "Mechanics Made Easy". Before World War I Meccano had developed close connections with Märklin, which manufactured the Meccano construction system under licence in Germany and, in turn, supplied Meccano with accessories like steam engines. Just before the war, Meccano had planned to market a rather peculiar, small Märklin train, with a gauge of 26mm, under the name of Raylo, but plans had not got very far when war was declared. However, Hornby was still determined to enter the toy train market, and in 1920 the first Hornby trains were catalogued.

These early trains were rather crude, but they were packaged in

Hornby 2710, 1920 (C); Bassett-Lowke G.W.R. Mogul, 1925 (G); Hornby L.N.E.R. 2711, 1921 (E); Hornby Pullman coach and dining saloon, 1921 (E)

In the 1920s, Hornby was best known as a manufacturer of toy trains, and its products such as the locomotive with a shiny brass dome – a feature that had not been seen on real locomotives since before World War I – had considerable naïve appeal. Early Hornby trains can be taken apart and reassembled, like Meccano sets: a play feature of dubious value since virtually no one bothered to do it. The roofs of the coaches are also removable, although there is no interior detail. Like Hornby locomotives, Bassett-Lowke products such as the Mogul, although recognizable locomotives, were intended to be used as toys. The strong construction, simplified details and shiny finish enabled the Mogul to stand up to hard use on any toy railway. *P. Dunk Collection*

BELOW RIGHT Hornby L.M.S. Pullman set, 1925 (G)

The lovely imitation-leather box with the gold-embossed lettering and train emblem, together with the flawlessly gleaming contents, goes a long way to explain Hornby's success in selling its relatively expensive and rather simple gauge O train sets against cheaper and more sophisticated competition. Hornby was always good with colour and presentation, and the brass dome on the 2711 locomotive perfectly complements the rich red maroon paint, even though brass domes were not a feature on real-life L.M.S. locomotives. *Phillips*

BELOW Hornby Crawford's biscuits van, 1924 (F) ; Hornby Colman's mustard van, 1924 (G)

A large, well-organized group of collectors, such as the Hornby Collectors Association, all chasing a relatively small group of desirable trains, such as the Hornby private-owner wagons, will always force the price up. Although both of these vans are scarce, and the Colman's van exists in particularly small numbers, neither can be truly classed as rare, but their splendid colouring and gold lettering make them outstanding in any collection and a must for Hornby collectors. *Phillips*

beautifully embossed, gold-lettered cardboard boxes, which looked like leather. The trains inside the boxes were considerably less interesting, however. Hornby's original plan had been to sell a range of toy trains that could be taken apart and put together again, like the Meccano construction sets. So that this could be done, the trains were made up from rather simple, heavy metal stampings, held together with standard Meccano nuts and screws, and finished in enamel. The sets were relatively expensive, but the trains were under-detailed and looked primitive. The little gauge O brass-domed 0-4-0s and 4-4-0s had reasonable clockwork motors, but they were not entirely trouble-free. Worst of all, the idea that the trains should be constructional was a total failure. The system added considerably to the cost of manufacture but at the same time weakened the assemblies, and no one ever took the trains apart or put them together again – there was no point, the component parts could not be used to build anything different.

Inferior products have always tested the mettle of marketing departments, and Hornby accepted the challenge with a truly inspired sales programme, which included a yearly catalogue, *The Hornby Book of Trains*. Hornby had looked at the boy-oriented colour catalogues published by American manufacturers, realized how important they were for stimulating the imagination and improved upon them. In addition to details about the train sets, Hornby catalogues included a lot of information on real trains, written in an informative, lively and non-patronizing style. The catalogues were supported by a monthly maga-

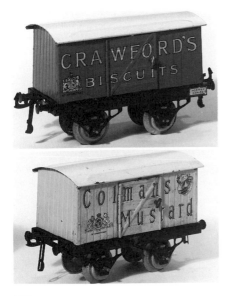

zine, which was edited to the same formula. Both publications used striking colour covers by leading artists. These marketing ploys were successful in selling large numbers of toy trains, and Hornby worked hard to improve its line.

The unsuccessful constructional system was phased out in the mid-1920s in favour of the more conventional Nuremberg-style tab and slot assembly process. Hornby did not make much use of lithographic printing for its locomotives and rolling stock, although all its stations, engine sheds and other buildings were lithographed. Following Lionel's example, Hornby used heavy enamel and bright colours, which meant that a comprehensive range could be produced with a minimum of fixed overhead cost. Transfers, largely gold, were used for the lettering and decoration. How much Hornby relied upon the German toy industry for its products is a matter for speculation, but at least one locomotive in the Hornby line was made by Bing. It is possible that the production machinery, tools and dies might have been designed and made in Germany. Certainly, there is a definite "Nuremberg look" to the revised Hornby trains.

Electricity was cautiously approached by Hornby, and the Metropolitan Railway electric outline locomotive, introduced in 1925, was the firm's sole electrically-powered example until the end of the 1920s. This locomotive, whose design owed a lot to American toy train practice, was a 0-4-0 masquerading as a twin-bogie electric. The body had a well-detailed, lithographed finish, brightened up with a considerable amount

Hornby Metropolitan set, 1925 (H)
For its first gauge O, electrically powered locomotive, Hornby used as a prototype the recently introduced electric Bo-Bo of the Metropolitan Railway, reducing its eight wheels to four. The general design and styling of the locomotives is similar to the American products of Lionel and Ives, even to the use of brass surrounds for the windows. Extensive use of lithography was another unusual feature of this set, and the locomotive was the only large Hornby engine to have a lithographed body. The coaches were extremely well made, and they were unique, among Hornby's large coaches, with their combination of lithography and punched-out windows.
Phillips

of gleaming brass detail, in the manner of Lionel. It was a curious locomotive, and its styling was unique in the range of Hornby locomotives.

During the 1920s the standard Hornby toy train system was cheerful, brightly coloured and attractive. A full range of accessories was listed, and the giant, double-tracked Hornby engine shed, which continued in production until World War II, was the finest lithographed building made by any toy train manufacturer.

In general, Hornby was not export minded, and a short-lived foray into the American market was quickly abandoned. France appeared to be a better prospect, and French outline locomotives and rolling stock appeared in Hornby catalogues. Eventually, a factory was established at Bobigny, France, which in time developed its own, separate product line. One of Hornby's first French locomotives was a Nord 4-6-2 Pacific, cut down to a 4-4-2 and sold with two wagons-lits coaches. Ironically, this French locomotive, painted and lettered for the L.M.S., L.N.E.R., Great Western Railway or Southern Railway, became Hornby's most popular large locomotive.

By the end of the 1920s Hornby had phased out its earlier, toy-like locomotives, with their polished brass domes, and added more realistic models to its system. Electricity was gradually becoming more popular. In 1928–9, Hornby had one electric train on offer; the next year saw three electrics in the catalogue and in 1931–2 the number was up to four, out of a total of 19 different locomotives.

At the end of the 1920s, four, extremely fine, scale outline 4-4-0 locomotives were quietly introduced. Initially all-clockwork, these locomotives went on to become the stars of the 1930s Hornby system.

In sharp contrast to Hornby's confident marketing and sales successes, Bassett-Lowke was in the doldrums for the greater part of the 1920s. The image that Bassett-Lowke had cultivated in previous years – that of a discerning manufacturer of fine scale models – did not help to sell toy trains, and Bassett-Lowke could not address the boy enthusiasts as easily as Hornby. The Bassett-Lowke product line for the first part of the 1920s was an uncoordinated amalgam of Bing trains and left-over Carette and Märklin items, filled out with English-made, cottage-industry accessories, manufactured primarily from wood; few new items were introduced. Bing's few gauge I and gauge O high-quality locomotives were largely left over from the brilliant pre-war period. W.J. Bassett-Lowke himself blamed the slump on the emergence of radio as the new fashionable hobby. The British firm of Winteringham became a new manufacturing sub-contractor for Bassett-Lowke and injected some life into the line by introducing a rather ponderous series of 2-6-0 Moguls in gauges I and O. A cheap but popular locomotive, called the *Duke of York*, initiated a long-running series of lithographed 4-4-0s.

Gamage's interest in toy trains declined dramatically in the 1920s, and Märklin's 4-4-2 North British Atlantic, 4-6-2 *Flying Scotsman* in steam, and the 4-6-4T *Stephenson* tank engine were dropped not long

Bassett-Lowke L.M.S. travelling post office, 1923 (D)

After World War I, Bing acquired a few of the tools and dies from the defunct Carette company and updated two of the coach types – the travelling post office and the 12-wheeled diner – to the new L.M.S. colours. The gauge I coach shown here and a gauge O equivalent were manufactured exclusively for Bassett-Lowke for a few years, a pale shadow of the former extensive Carette selection. The mail-bag apparatus will pick up and deposit miniature mail-bags on the fly, using a special rail section. *Phillips*

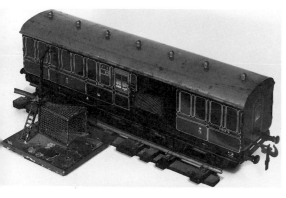

Bassett-Lowke L.N.E.R. Mogul 1927 (F)
By the late 1920s, a firm called Winteringham had an arrangement to manufacture locomotives exclusively for Basset-Lowke. The first production was a group of Moguls in gauge O, followed by the introduction of the gauge I Moguls in 1926. Originally designed as steamers, the Moguls are somewhat simplified and over-large for gauge O. The gauge II N.E.R. engine, powered by an electric motor, is probably the most successful design of the lot. Moguls were also made in the liveries of the L.M.S., G.W.R. and S.R.
Sotherby's, London

Bassett-Lowke L.M.S. Mogul, 1926 (F)
The first locomotives designed and manufactured for Bassett-Lowke by the firm of Winteringham were steam models for the four major railways. Although the designs were originally for steam, both electric and clockwork versions were also sold; however, the proportions remained oversized and the construction was very heavy, with coarse detailing. The production life of these locomotives was very long, and the last fifty engines were L.M.S. steam Moguls, updated for British Railways.
Sotheby's, London

Bassett-Lowke L.M.S. Compound, 1928 (E)
The lithographed gauge O Bassett-Lowke locomotives represented an attempt to acquire a portion of the medium-range market that had become increasingly dominated by Hornby. Unfortunately for Bassett-Lowke, at approximately the same time Hornby also introduced a Compound that was better finished, more attractive and cheaper. In spite of this disadvantage and in spite of some peculiar colours, large numbers of the Bassett-Lowke Compounds were sold and today they are relatively common and cheaper than the Hornby version. *Sotheby's, London*

BELOW Märklin L.N.E.R. *Flying Scotsman*, 1924 (L)
In the mid-1920s, Märklin updated its gauge I Great Western Railway steam Pacific and produced a gigantic L.N.E.R. locomotive, which was usually called *Flying Scotsman*. However, Märklin must have had a few old name-plates left over, so that the L.N.E.R engine in the photo has the G.W.R. name-plate, *The Great Bear*. Too large to be just a toy and too awkward to be a scale model, the L.N.E.R. Pacific was not a good seller, and the remaining stocks were dumped on the market in the mid-1930s at a fraction of their original price.
Sotheby's, London

Bing for Bassett-Lowke L.M.S. composite brake, 1925 (D); Bing L.N.E.R. coach, 1925 (D); Bing for Bassett-Lowke L.M.S. corridor coach, 1925 (D); Bassett-Lowke G.W.R. Mogul, 1927 (G)
The last Bing series of gauge O lithographed coaches made for Bassett-Lowke was superbly designed, and the sides of the coaches were printed with great precision. After the break-up of Bing, Bassett-Lowke was forced to manufacture its own lithographed coaches, but the quality of the Bing rolling stock was never equalled. The L.N.E.R. coach is a Bing freelance effort, which carried the livery of continental as well as British railways. The roof shape is continental and is hinged to allow access to a beautifully detailed interior. The G.W.R. locomotive is one of four Bassett-Lowke Mogul designs representing the major British railways.
Sotheby's, London

after their introduction. By the end of the 1920s, Märklin had ceased to supply Gamage's, and Gamage's remaining stocks of Märklin locomotives were dumped on the English market at below wholesale prices.

Bing, alone among the major German toy makers, continued to provide cheap toy train sets for the British market in competition to Hornby. Bing sets were quite good during the 1920s, but the firm's marketing was not in the same league as Hornby's, and Bing generally lacked "image". However, Bing kept trying, and at the end of the decade an entire new range of locomotives with newly designed and extremely powerful clockwork motors was released. In cooperation with Bassett-Lowke, Bing produced the innovative "table-top" railway, which was half the size of gauge O, with a rail spacing of 16mm and a scale of 4mm to the foot; it was called "OO" gauge. The little locomotives, wagons and coaches were pure Nuremberg, and the track was laid on embossed tin bases. Appealing as it was, the new gauge was not very successful, even though the locomotives were available in either clockwork or electric.

The general lack of interest in the "table-top" sets stifled development, and the sets remained unchanged, although they lingered in the catalogues for several years. Judging from the design of the locomotives, the OO systems were intended solely for Britain, but the Nuremberg methods of folded, lithographed tin did not work well in this small size, and the results were too clumsy and dwarfish to be taken seriously.

During the 1920s, several small firms sprang up in Britain. They offered scale-model railway supplies, which competed with Bassett-Lowke's range, but most of them were extremely small efforts and lasted only a short time. One exception, however, was the enterprising Leeds Model Company (L.M.C.), founded by R.F. Steadman. Leeds aimed to provide, at a competitive price, a gauge O railway system that had a reasonable scale outline. Rolling stock was largely wooden, with decorative details printed on the paper sides. Locomotives were made from simplified pressings and die-castings. It was an attractive system, but, unfortunately, it did not survive well. The wooden bodies tended to warp and rot, the paper sides wrinkled and peeled off, and the zinc die-castings fatigued badly. As a result, items produced by Leeds are today

Bing G.N.R. 4-4-0 "DI", 1920 (F)
The Great Northern Railway class 4-4-0 "DI" was probably the nicest of the gauge O cheaper Bing locomotives. Although the "DI" was all lithographed and designed to sell as a cheap engine, the printing, colour and proportions were all extremely good and showed that a reasonable model could be made to sell for a competitive price. *Sotherby's, London*

Bing for Bassett-Lowke M.R. "2P" class, 1921 (H)
One of the few new gauge I designs introduced after World War I, the Bing "2P" was a great improvement on the similar model by Märklin, although, with its large boiler and forward-mounted smoke-box, it compares unfavourably with Bing's own, extremely graceful M.R. Compound. Bing's safety valve is a sturdy construction of brass parts and is practically unbreakable, unlike the frail lead casting of Märklin's locomotive. *Christie's, London*

CENTRE Bing for Bassett–Lowke, freelance 4-6-0, 1922 (I)
This large and complex gauge II locomotive was the high point of Bing's steam engine development and one of the last series done for Bassett-Lowke. The tender carried both water and fuel, and a pump, worked from the cab, kept the boiler well supplied with water. The large outside lever, also worked from the cab, reversed the direction of travel. Unfortunately the locomotive illustrated here has had its neat Bing safety valve replaced by a large and clumsy steam cock. *Sotheby's, London*

Bing L.N.W.R. *George V*, 1920 (E)
By the 1920s Bing had transformed its soldered and hand-painted *George V* locomotive made for Bassett-Lowke, into a lithographed and tabbed-together version suitable for mass production. It was an extremely popular locomotive and thousands were sold, so that today a collector would have no trouble in acquiring one. However, most of these engines had a hard life, and few would be in the same pristine condition as the one in the photograph. *Sotheby's, London*

Bing L.M.S. *Apollo*, 1925 (D)
The *Apollo* was a 4-wheeled variant of the many changes Bing rang on its basic *George V* styling. The square base to the chimney is an indication of its L.N.W.R. derivation. The 0-4-0s like the *Apollo* were strong, with realistic details and beautifully running mechanisms, but Bing merchandising was no match for Hornby, and Bing gradually lost its share of the British market. *Sotheby's, London*

greatly undervalued, although surviving stock in good condition is very appealing.

On the other hand, sturdy rolling stock and locomotives were the hallmark of the highly individual Bowman Company, of Norwich, England, and many examples of the firm's products exist today. Bowman wanted to provide a good toy; it was not much interested in scale models. Steam was Bowman's strong point and all its toy gauge O locomotives were steam powered. Although they ran on gauge O track, Bowman trains were closer to gauge I in scale and the passenger coaches were, in fact, longer than most gauge I coaches, a full 17in (43cm).

Bowman locomotives, with their big boilers and rugged, simple construction, were magnificent runners, and surviving examples are usually badly scorched from hard use. Bowman freight stock was attractively but crudely constructed of wood, and the wheel standards were a throw-back to 1900. The attractive lithographed sides, which featured opening compartment doors, were simply nailed on to the

only piece of passenger rolling stock, and the handsome, lithographed sides were decorated in the liveries of L.N.W.R., L.N.E.R. and L.M.S, The tank locomotive was available in two different sizes, both gauge O. The larger size, not shown here, was a better visual match for the coach. Bar Knight made a variety of rather crude-looking locomotives similar in styling to Bowman products, and a small, more refined series of lithographed rolling stock, in the manner of Carette. Bar Knight locomotives were available in steam, clockwork and electric, but even this variety was not enough to overcome customer resistance, and the company quickly vanished. *Courtesy London Toy and Model Museum; P. Carlson Collection*

wooden frames of the Bowman coaches. The goods wagons were decorated by hand, with a drawing pen, which must have resulted in a slow rate of production. In spite of their crudity, the Bowman products were popular, and, today, Bowman locomotives exist in reasonable numbers, although the rolling stock, especially the goods wagons, is relatively scarce.

The Glasgow firm of Bar Knight made a serious attempt to provide a range of commercial toy railways, but although they were smaller and closer to scale, the locomotives appeared to be as crude as those produced by Bowman. Judging from the few that exist today, they must have been poor sellers. Occasionally an item of lithographed rolling stock appears, which suggests that the firm was thinking of mass production, but definite information on the extent of the Bar Knight range is practically non-existent, and this little-known Scottish company is very much on the periphery of British toy train manufacture.

French manufacturers benefited from the decline in German exports

BELOW LEFT Märklin Paris-Orleans El electric, 1920 (H) ·
One of the new locomotives that Märklin had ready to sell at the beginning of the 1920s was this model of a French electric locomotive, in 8-wheel and 4-wheel configurations. Both versions – in gauge I as well as gauge O – were extremely large and over-scale. The construction was solid and heavy, and every hand-painted rivet was shadowed in black, to add depth. Surprisingly, the pantograph is just a plain, non-working stamping. The gauge I example illustrated is a high-voltage model, which was run on a potentially lethal 110-220 volts. *Sotheby's, New York*

BELOW RIGHT Märklin G.N.R. 2-4-0 tank, 1925 (H)
The popularity of this rather plain gauge I tank locomotive derives from its appearance in the German catalogues

during the 1920s, although Märklin still had a good grip on the luxury end of the market with its P.L.M. Pacific and new PO El steeple-cab electric locomotives. J.E.P. was beginning to make very advanced trains, and Rossignol, which had introduced electric trains into its range *c.*1919, was still a strong contender in the market for cheap train sets. Robert Marescot offered a scale Nord Pacific with scale coaches to match, and this expensive, hand-built series catered to a gradually emerging group of French enthusiasts. Later, the Marescot line was taken over and continued by M. Fournereau.

Hornby, too, was making an impression on the French toy-train market with its electric-drive Nord *Riviera* set, produced at its factory at Bobigny. L.R. (Le Rapide), a firm that became an important manufacturer in the 1930s, (see page 137), started in the late 1920s with a line of trains made primarily from die-castings.

over a number of years with the designation "TMN". To the German collector, it represents a rare and difficult engine to find. The British collector is less enthusiastic because the

2-4-0T wheel arrangement was not common on prototype railways. The particular one pictured must have hardly ever been run as there are no scratches around the keyhole. *Christie's, London*

Fischer L.N.E.R. train set, 1925 (E)
Who said that gauge O had to be large? This tiny Fischer train set is shorter and will take tighter curves than most modern HO/OO trains. Although the

set is very economically made, with stamped drivers and the simplest of couplers, the lithography and lettering is carefully done and the major style characteristics of an L.N.E.R. coach are

reproduced faithfully on the little 4-wheelers. A set such as this is quite rare but still very inexpensive, proving that rarity alone will not make the price high. *Phillips*

MÄRKLIN REORGANIZES

In Germany, the 1920s was a time of reassessment. The collapse of Märklin's ambitious pre-war export programme had shaken the great Göppingen company. The post-war catalogues were filled with left-over export items and peculiar locomotives made from parts of American designs; American rolling stock and British locomotives were repainted with continental liveries, which Märklin hoped would appeal to German buyers. Never at a loss for long, however, Märklin, the mainspring and inspiration of the German toy industry, began to move again. Observing how effective the manufacturers' customer-oriented catalogues had been in the United States and the similar success Hornby enjoyed in establishing its image in Britain, Märklin started its own series of customer catalogues, which became all-colour by the end of the 1920s. The company drastically trimmed its vast and rather unmanageable pre-

Märklin S.R. Stephenson, 1925 (K)
The gauge O Southern Railway tank engine was based on the same 6-coupled mechanism that was used for the P.L.M. Pacific, and was, in fact, an up-date of their pre-war L.N.W.R. Bowen-Cooke 6-coupled tank engine. Because this locomotive was included in occasional Märklin continental catalogues with the designation "TK", it has become a particular favourite of continental collectors. The general styling and finish is more closely related to Märklin's pre-war series for Gamage's than to the company's emerging *Reichsbahn* line. *Phillips*

Märklin wagon lit coach, 1920 (J)
The 53cm (10.88in) gauge I coach series was designed to accompany the P.L.M. Pacific but did not appear until after World War I. These coaches were the largest in the Märklin catalogue for several years and, although ungainly, were certainly impressive. Their large size meant that an interior was a definite requirement, but, unfortunately, the example shown has none, and therefore the value of this coach would be almost halved. *Sotheby's, London*

Märklin flask wagon with *Bremserhaus*, 1923 (G); Märklin aeroplane wagon, 1923 (H); Märklin wine wagon, 1923 (F)
These three gauge O wagons, which were also made in gauge I, were among the more interesting wagons manufactured in the 1920s, although the Bleriot-type aeroplane seems to be rather old fashioned for the period. The wings detach and store in slots alongside the fuselage, but the vertical tailplane appears to be missing. The wine wagon is quite rare because examples are seldom seen with French markings. *Christie's, London*

Märklin PO E1, 1919 (H); Märklin Gotthard, 1921 (L)

Electric outline locomotives played a major part in Märklin's recovery after World War I. These two heavy electrics in gauge O were the largest in the catalogue in the early 1920s. The *Gotthard* is loosely based on the lines of a Swiss locomotive, and it is one of the most elaborate models in the Märklin range, especially with the fearsome array of oversize lamps at the front. The PO E1 is supposed to be a French steeple-cab locomotive for the Paris–Orleans railway. This locomotive is considerably oversize for gauge O, and its great width must have presented problems for the toy stations and tunnels through which it was supposed to pass. *D. Burt Collection*

war range and stopped production of most of the non-train toys. Only gauge O and gauge I remained in the catalogue, and the emphasis was put on realism and scale models taken from prototypes operating on the German *Reichsbahn* and the Swiss railway.

Märklin catalogue covers and box-lids tended to show scenes of intense industrial effort, rendered with romantic gloom. The number of accessories was reduced, but Märklin still had a larger range than any other German manufacturer. Many of the accessories were electrically operated, and Märklin concentrated on electrical sophistication, designing the new range specifically to appeal to the German and Swiss home market. No effort was spared in making the products convincing as models: Märklin's speciality, the large, elaborate stations, were still catalogued, but the firm took care to ensure that all the accessories were more realistic and better matched visually.

Märklin passenger station, 1926 (H)
This attractive medium-sized station shows how well Märklin was able to use the pressings and details from the huge Leipzig station to make a whole range of lesser stations. Like most of Märklin's 1920s range of accessories, the colouring is a rather uninspired tan, in contrast to the vivid pre-war colours, and the styling is much less fantastic.
Sotheby's, New York

This coordination of the range also applied to the locomotives, and a coherent series began to emerge. Customers could start with a cheap 0-4-0 shunting engine and work up to an expensive electric or 4-4-2 Atlantic, without having to drop the 0-4-0. Instead of concentrating on the top end of the market alone, Märklin provided a complete progression of prices, within its own product range. This intelligent rationalization of its own toy railway system, the good design and the maintenance of high standards of quality began to work, and, by the end of the 1920s, Märklin was once again the strongest German toy train company.

The other German manufacturers were not so fortunate. Bing, which had started up again strongly in the period just after World War I, had been drifting, seemingly without direction, and, by the end of the 1920s, the sprawling, uncoordinated range was becoming unattractive to customers. The Bing family, which had been the driving force during the successful collaboration with Bassett-Lowke, was no longer in charge,

ABOVE Bing electric set, 1928 (E)
One of Bing's last locomotives for gauge O, this plain little engine was in production until the company's demise in 1932. The two coaches are equally uninteresting, and the lack of registration between the window punching and the lithography, combined with the general lack of finish of the set, is evidence of Bing's sad decline from its previous high standards. *Sotheby's, London*

ABOVE RIGHT Bing 4-4-0 Compound, 1925 (H)
First introduced in 1912, the pudgy and awkward Bing Continental Compound express locomotive was in production for almost two decades. This particular gauge I example is post-1925, as indicated by the late "BW" trademark. There were many different finishes for this locomotive, including a beautiful blue with red lining and a black one with extensive lining in gold and red. Missing one electric headlamp, this locomotive would have additional difficulty running with its tender back to front. *Sotheby's, London*

and the lack of centralized control caused serious financial problems for Bing. When the firm's finances began to fail, no loyal group of Bing fans rallied round to rescue it, and time began to run out for the famous Nuremberg firm.

Somehow, the moribund Plank company had survived into the 1920s, still including in its catalogues a few ancient locomotives from the turn of the century. But by the end of the decade, Plank had ceased trading. Doll and Falk occasionally produced unexciting, but cheap, train sets, but the main suppliers of cheap trains were Karl Bub and Kraus. Issmayer, never very visible at the best of times, finally disappeared for good in the early 1930s. Since this early and influential company does not seem to be survived by any existing catalogue, its history can only be inferred from a few remaining examples and the appearance of its products in other manufacturers' catalogues.

By the close of the 1920s, the old, international aspect of toy trains had virtually disappeared and most manufacturers had retreated behind their national boundaries. The long-term result of this retreat was greater concentration on national railways and an increase in realism. The old toy train was slowly being replaced by the scale model.

6

DEPRESSION AND RECOVERY: THE RISE OF MINIATURE GAUGE 1930–45

In the 1930s the economic and political climate in both Europe and the United States worsened. Nothing was more unexpected than the American Depression that began with the Wall Street Crash in 1929. All the American toy train makers had been accelerating their development programmes throughout the 1920s, and companies continued to offer new, even more *de luxe* trains even after the Crash, when the market for luxury toy trains was shrinking rapidly.

Ives was the first casualty when, in 1932, Lionel withdrew its support. Lionel had entered the 1930s with ambitious plans to overwhelm American toy train buyers with a new range of super *de luxe* Standard gauge sets. The largest electric, the 12-wheeled 381, had come on to the market in 1928, but the huge, 21in (53cm) *State* passenger coaches did not reach the shops until 1929. That same year also saw the introduction of a series of new steam outline locomotives, the first new steam-type trains from Lionel in over twenty years. These locomotives marked Lionel's return to the more traditional form of the toy train. They were made in the same way as the firm's electric locomotives – largely from heavy steel stampings with ornamental brass trim – but they were notable for the use of die-castings for such parts as cylinders, frames, boiler fronts and other details, the first time that Lionel had used die-castings. The new steamers were more complex than the electrics and cost more to manufacture. There were four basic types in Standard gauge, ranging from a 2-4-0 up to the massive 400E, 4-4-4, which pulled the *Blue Comet*, Lionel's entirely new and most famous toy train, which was first offered for sale in 1930. Lionel added more Standard gauge coaches, the *Stephen Girard* set, to its line in 1932.

In addition to the new trains it was now offering for sale under its own name, Lionel had also financed all the new trains for the Ives line, in both Standard and gauge O. All these trains had been designed during the boom that the United States had enjoyed in the 1920s, and their exuberant, colourful, Italian styling contrasted sharply with the bleak, Depression gloom. Lionel was in trouble: too many Standard gauge trains were chasing too few dollars.

American Flyer was facing similar problems, and in 1936 it unceremoniously dropped its Wide gauge line, even though its gauge O trains were old fashioned and the range needed overhauling. In the mid-1930s American Flyer was in dire financial straits and close to going out of business. The Depression, and trouble with fatigue in the die-castings, put Dorfan out of business, and, in 1929, Boucher decided to concentrate

Lionel Mickey Mouse hand-car, 1934 (H)
In 1934 the United States was in the depths of the Depression, and Lionel was in receivership: if its business did not improve, Lionel would go bankrupt. Desperate times called for desperate remedies, and the hand-car series was an attempt to capture part of the cheap novelty toy market – quite a come down for the mighty Lionel corporation. The inexpensive gauge O clockwork hand-cars were propelled by Santa Claus, Peter Rabbit, Mickey and Minnie Mouse and Donald Duck, accompanied by a recumbent Pluto. The hand-cars were an enormous success, but the low profit margins meant that their sales alone could not save Lionel. The success of the Union Pacific streamliner played a far larger part. Despite the popularity of the hand-cars and the Mickey Mouse circus tent, Lionel did not follow up its success, and the novelty toy market was left to firms like Marx. *Sotheby's, New York*

Elettren FS 2-D-2, 1955 (G); Märklin HS 66, 1935 (L); Lionel U.P. *City of Portland*, 1934 (G); J.E.P. Nord *Golden Arrow* and Pullman baggage wagon, 1936 (G)
The Elettren electric, shown with this group of gauge O trains, clearly demonstrates the comparatively large size of these post-war Italian trains. The Lionel *City of Portland* (which is lacking the middle coach so that it could be squeezed into the photograph) was extremely important, partly because it was the first train to be released after the design office had been moved back from Italy, and partly because the sales success of this streamliner saved the company from bankruptcy. The Märklin electric HS 66 was a popular large electric, and the realistic styling of its sheet-metal construction was characteristic of Märklin's production in the mid-1930s. On the other hand the Nord *Golden Arrow* Pacific was still very much a toy, although it was one of J.E.P.'s finest efforts, and a set complete with the handsome, lithographed Pullmans is highly regarded by collectors. *Courtesy London Toy and Model Museum; D. Burt Collection*

**Lionel "Hell Gate" bridge, 1928 (H);
Lionel *Blue Comet* set, 1931 (M)**
It was unfortunate for Lionel that the market for expensive Standard gauge sets disappeared just when the biggest and best Standard gauge train sets appeared on the market. The beautiful blue 400E locomotive and the three handsome 12-wheeled passenger cars, complete with interiors and lights, which made up the legendary *Blue Comet* set, probably constituted the finest toy train ever marketed by Lionel. Although the passenger coaches are smaller than the giant *State* coaches, they had better proportions, and the 400E was the largest and most impressive locomotive produced by Lionel. As a testimonial to the set's popularity, even during hard times the *Blue Comet* remained in production until the end of the 1930s and the end of Standard gauge. *Sotheby's, New York*

on model ships, finally retiring the range of big, Voltamp-based trains it had been making.

By the mid-1930s, Lionel, which had not shown a profit for four years, was in receivership. Since it was no longer economically advantageous for Lionel's design and die-work to be carried out in Italy, the Naples works was sold, thus ending the era of Italian design that had set the style, not only for Lionel but for all other American toy trains.

In the mid-1930s, however, toy train manufacturers in the United States received an unexpected boost. Air travel, although increasing in popularity, was still the preserve of wealthy dare-devils; road travel, along poorly maintained highways, was difficult. Most people travelled by train, and the new streamlined trains caught the public's imagination in a way that earlier trains had not. The new streamliners, as they were known, were shiny symbols of hope for millions struggling out of the Depression. Lionel capitalized on the mood of optimism by producing (*c.*1934) a very good model of the Union Pacific *City of Portland*. With this train, Lionel inaugurated a popular series of streamliners, all of which proved to be good sellers, and the sales of these trains pulled the firm out of receivership.

Standard gauge was no longer used by any of the American toy train

makers. The streamliners, like all the other new trains, were made in gauge O. In the absence of a *de luxe* gauge, Lionel developed three different sizes of gauge O. The smallest size, which was used for a range of cheap sets, was known as O-27, because the track had a radius of 27in (69cm). The largest size used a track radius of 74in (1m 88cm), and the middle size had a radius of 31in (79cm). Lionel increased the number of streamliners it offered, until there were five altogether. The steam outline locomotives that Lionel continued to produce were still based upon the Italian designs using die-castings and brass trim.

American Flyer, observing Lionel's success with its range of streamliners, hurriedly produced an extensive group of its own. Unfortunately, American Flyer streamliners, although quite attractive, did not seem to be as good value as Lionel's, and they were not a sales success. At this low point in American Flyer's affairs, A.C. Gilbert, a wealthy toy manufacturer, stepped in and bought the company in 1938, moving it from Chicago to New Haven, Connecticut. Under its new management, the firm scrapped its old trains, and a totally new line was designed from scratch. These new toy trains were made in gauge O, but they were to a much smaller scale, even smaller than Lionel's O-27 range. However, the quality of the new American Flyer trains was much higher than those made by Lionel for O-27, and the finely detailed die-castings and good proportions were a great success with the public. With increased sales, American Flyer was reborn.

Lionel, too, at this time began to consider using die-castings as a means of reducing the manufacturing costs of its steam outline locomotives. To test the feasibility of the scheme, Lionel invited a Swedish-American firm of tool and die manufacturers to design a gauge O fine scale model of the New York Central 4-6-4 "Hudson" and some matching freight cars. The number of scale-model enthusiasts throughout the country was growing, and Lionel wanted to use the "Hudson" to

Lionel signal, 1936 (B); Lionel U.P. *City of Denver*, 1936 (F)
The huge success of its large gauge O *City of Portland* streamliner, introduced in 1934, encouraged Lionel to market an entire range of streamliner sets. The *City of Denver* was probably the most attractive of the smaller sets and featured the same articulated coach construction that characterized the larger streamliner series. Extensive use of die-casting and sheet-steel construction resulted in a toy train that was almost indestructible. *Phillips*

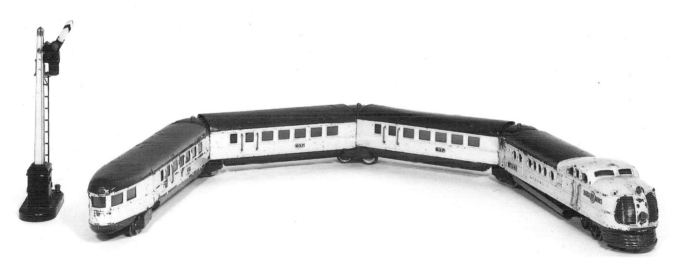

Lionel Pennsylvania Railroad 0-6-0, 1939 (H)

Building model railroads had become a popular hobby in the United States in the 1930s, but there were very few ready-to-run models, and those that were available tended to be very expensive. The accurate gauge O Pennsylvania switcher, along with a scale "Hudson" and a handful of die-cast freight cars, was produced by Lionel to test the size of the scale model market. Unfortunately, the war put a stop to this promising development, and the Lionel super-scale series was never

revived. The models that were produced, unequalled in their fidelity to detail and proportion, are a tantalizing reminder of what Lionel could have produced had it decided to manufacture a scale model line after the war. *Sotheby's, New York*

American Flyer Milwaukee Road *Hiawatha*, 1936 (H)
In the 1930s, the Chicago-based firm of American Flyer tried very hard to revive its flagging sales by issuing an extensive range of "streamliners" in gauge O. The attractive *Hiawatha* was probably the best one, but, even its advanced die-cast; sheet-steel construction could not save American Flyer from collapse. *P. Dunk Collection*

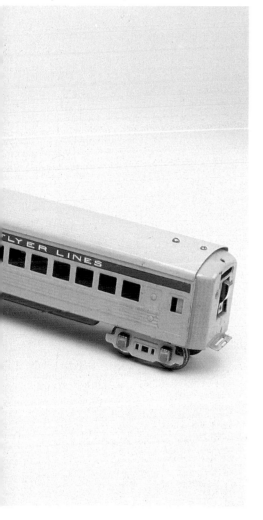

investigate the extent of the hobby market and also to provide publicity for a projected series of die-cast, steam outline locomotives. The magnificent model was such a success that Lionel recovered the tooling costs in the first year. No other toy train manufacturer had ever produced a locomotive in gauge O to such a high standard of realism, and it is still a standard that has rarely been equalled.

Encouraged by the success of the "Hudson", the company brought out an 0-6-0 Pennsylvania engine to the same standard. These two superb locomotives prepared the way for the new Lionel die-cast look, and from 1937 onwards, all Lionel locomotives were made from semi-scale, chunky die-castings, with lots of moulded detail. The robust and colourful Italian look of the 1920s was gone for good.

With Ives gone and American Flyer aiming for the quality market, the well-established New York toy making firm of Louis Marx began to increase its business at the cheaper end of the toy train market. Marx was best known as a manufacturer of tin-plate novelty toys, but it also made cheap clockwork trains. Because of the firm's policy of never issuing a catalogue, a complete list of Marx trains is not available and many interesting items remain to be discovered by the determined Marx collector. The most desirable of all known Marx products, however, is the ill-fated "Bunny Express". Produced for the 1936 Easter season, this was a clockwork, rabbit-shaped locomotive, pulling a train of candy-filled open wagons. It was an instant sales flop, which ensured its scarcity, and today it is the most sought-after of all Marx trains.

BASSETT-LOWKE RECOVERS

In Britain in the 1930s Bassett-Lowke found a more encouraging climate for its enthusiast-oriented range. A selection of large, powerful, British locomotives, concentrating on the 6-coupled types, was manufactured. Two gauge O locomotives – the 4-6-2 *Flying Scotsman* and the 4-6-0 *Royal Scot* – were made for Bassett-Lowke by Winteringham, c.1935, and they were the finest locomotives ever made in the "Nuremberg style". Although designed as expensive, precision scale models, both locomotives were made from stamped, lithographed parts, assembled with tabs and slots. Winteringham continued to make both locomotives for Bassett-Lowke in large numbers for over thirty years, and they are still among the most attractive locomotives ever offered for sale. To accompany these large locomotives, Winteringham also made a group of more modest 0-6-0s and 4-4-0s. The remaining locomotives in the Bassett-Lowke catalogue were made in the traditional, craftsman's way by soldering, hand forming and hand painting; the resulting slow production meant that these locomotives were much more expensive than those made from lithographed tin.

For a brief period in the 1930s, after the demise of Bing c.1932, Bassett-Lowke resumed its ties with Märklin. A couple of German outline engines were added to the list, as well as four gauge O German-made, British outline locomotives. These four locomotives, which were

Bassett-Lowke L.M.S. *Conqueror*, 1936 (I)

In the 1930s, Bassett-Lowke concentrated on gauge O and produced a very fine group of high-grade locomotives, based upon their refined 6-coupled mechanism, which was available as either clockwork or electric. This particular example has been super-detailed, and such things as boiler wash-out plugs have been added. It is always difficult to tell if the super-detailing was done at the factory or not. Frequently, Bassett-Lowke locomotives were returned to have repairs or to be repainted, altered or upgraded. The factory often put the job out to an independent craftsman who worked on his own, and the results varied. *Phillips*

Basset-Lowke L.M.S. 0-6-0T tank engine, 1933 (F)

The 6-coupled tank engine was quite popular because of the excellent Bassett-Lowke mechanism, and because no other British outline locomotives with the same wheel configuration were produced by rival manufacturers. Although it was at the more inexpensive end of the Bassett-Lowke gauge O range, the standard tank was still an expensive locomotive and consequently treasured by its owners. Most of the locomotives that turn up today, therefore, are in excellent condition. *Sotheby's, London*

Bassett-Lowke L.N.E.R. *Arsenal*, super-detailed, 1936 (J); Bassett-Lowke L.N.E.R. *Arsenal*, 1936 (I)

The *de luxe* Bassett-Lowke gauge O locomotives were of soldered construction and carefully hand painted. However, the rather low level of detailing did not satisfy every customer, and super-detailed versions could be ordered, at extra cost. It is difficult to determine whether or not the work has been done by Bassett-Lowke itself or by some later owner. On the super-detailed *Arsenal*, one of a series named after famous football clubs, the painting of the football is much superior to the standard model, and centre driver flanges have been added as well as wash-out plugs and a whistle. *Phillips and Sotheby's, London*

exclusive to Bassett-Lowke, were a 4-6-0 "King" class, a 4-6-0 5XP, a 2-6-4 tank and a "Schools" class 4-4-0. This series proved to be the last gauge O locomotives to be produced by the Germans for the British.

By the mid-1930s, locomotives in gauge I and the other large gauges were attracting very little interest, and Bassett-Lowke catalogues merely listed old stock. All interest was focused on the new, sleek, gauge O models, especially the two advanced streamliners, the Gresley-designed L.N.E.R. 4-6-2 Pacific *Silver Link* and the L.M.S. 4-6-2 Pacific *Coronation* by Stanier. Bassett-Lowke's catalogue included a small selection of lithographed rolling stock, together with wooden wagons and hand-painted passenger coaches, made for Bassett-Lowke by the scale model firm of Exley. Since Exley applied the numbers and letters on these coaches by hand, the finish tended to vary from the outstandingly smart to the rather untidy. The usual wooden buildings and accessories rounded off Bassett-Lowke's stock. The overall effect of the locomotives and station accessories was that of a scale model rather than of a "toy" train, and people who had grown up with the bright and bouncy Hornby line found the Bassett-Lowke models slightly "cold" and unappealing.

By the 1930s, Hornby had fulfilled its early promise and a remarkably complete railway system, with a clearly identifiable style, was produced and marketed. Hornby managed to ensure that all its locomotives had improved scale looks, but it achieved this without sacrificing the basic toy values of colour and practicality. Passenger coaches, for example, were lithographed, and the windows were printed on to solid silver-coloured metal, which created an effect that was actually better than punched-

Bassett-Lowke L.M.S. *Coronation*, 1937 (M)

The streamlined Pacifics produced by Bassett-Lowke in gauge O in the 1930s are the most sought-after of all the Bassett-Lowke locomotives. Only two different types were made: the L.M.S. *Coronation* and the L.N.E.R., Gresley-designed A4. These locomotives were hand built in small batches and beautifully painted and lined, although the level of detailing was not high and such things as cab details were usually omitted. At twelve guineas to fourteen guineas, the price represented over twelve weeks' wages for an average working man at a time when a new car could be bought for £100. They were slow sellers and stocks were still on hand in the post-war years. *Phillips*

Hornby S.R. *Eton*, 1937 (J)

The Hornby Southern Railway *Eton* Schools-class locomotive was in a class by itself; in fact, it was the only locomotive classed as a No. 4, which was intended to be a group of improved No. 2 specials. By using the basic bodywork of the L.N.E.R. *Bramham Moor* and adding a new cab, smoke deflectors and a few brass pipes, Hornby was able to offer a *de luxe* new locomotive for very little extra cost in new tooling. The unsightly front bulb holder was eliminated from the electric version, which must have pleased the scale-minded Hornby enthusiasts, as well as making the *Eton* that much cheaper to produce. *Sotheby's London*

Hornby No. 2 Special Pullmans, 1935 (each Pullman E)

This pair of Pullmans is in the third and final variation of the paint schemes used for these elaborate gauge O passenger coaches. Superbly finished and rather elegantly proportioned, these coaches suffer from a lack of interior detailing, a deficiency that is hidden by the rather opaque window glazing, printed with table lamps. *Phillips*

Marx Easter rabbit train, 1936 (K)
This is the sort of toy train that makes the scale model enthusiast groan – an effect it also had on Louis Marx. Produced, against the wishes of Marx's advisers, for Easter 1936, it was a resounding flop, and Louis Marx forbade any mention of it within his hearing. It should have had more success because it is a charming toy, with real glass eyes, which could be either pink or blue, and madly thrashing hind legs. The hopper cars were originally sold filled with jelly beans. *Courtesy London Toy and Model Museum*

Bassett-Lowke B.R. *Duchess of Montrose,* 1950 (I); **Bassett-Lowke L.N.E.R.** *Melton Hall,* 1936 (I); **Bassett-Lowke G.W.R.** *Pendennis Castle,* 1939 (J); **Bassett-Lowke L.M.S.** *Princess Royal,* 1935 (I)
This selection of locomotives is from the Bassett-Lowke gauge O top-quality range, which spanned a period from the early 1930s to the end of the 1950s. The last examples, made in the 1950s, were largely the work of one craftsman, the late Vic Hunt. Because Bassett-Lowke locomotives in this range look so much better in pristine condition, collectors of these models tolerate a greater degree of restoration than would be acceptable on locomotives by other manufacturers. A total repaint, if done by a recognized expert such as Littledale of Brighton, does not seem to detract much from the value; in fact, the reverse is often true. *T. Morris Collection*

Hornby L.M.S. Compound, 1935(G); Hornby G.W.R. *County of Bedford*, 1935 (H); Hornby S.R. *Eton*, 1937 (J); Hornby L.N.E.R. *Bramham Moor*, 1935 (H)
The competitive pricing of these four nicely detailed locomotives by Hornby brought realistic railway construction within the reach of the average toy train buyer in the 1930s. Their good proportions, gleaming enamel finish and superior mechanisms have always been appreciated by British enthusiasts. Although not rare, the Hornby semi-scale "specials" are keenly sought after, and clean examples always bring a premium price. *D. Burt Collection*

Märklin steam Pacific, 1935 (M); Märklin G.W.R. *King George V*, 1935 (K); Märklin L.M.S. *Stanier tank*, 1935 (H); Märklin S.R. *Merchant Taylors*, 1934 (I)
During the 1930s, Märklin locomotives for gauge O were tremendously varied but always well made. The British outline locomotives, produced exclusively for Bassett-Lowke, were sold in tiny quantities, but reasonable numbers survive because their owners recognized the quality and took good care of them. The ungainly but complex German Pacific represents Märklin's final fling at producing a toy locomotive that could actually be operated by steam. Subsequent locomotives were almost all driven by electricity, although high quality clockwork was still available for the British market.
Courtesy London Toy and Model Museum; D. Burt Collection

through windows. With the exceptions of the cheap M.O. line and the electric Metropolitan, all of the locomotives were enamelled in bright colours, as was most of the rolling stock.

The four semi-scale 4-4-0s, which had first appeared in 1929, were joined in 1937 by a super-detailed Southern Railway 4-4-0 *Eton*. Hornby's S.R. *Eton* was remarkable for its accuracy compared with the prototype. All these locomotives were available with electric motors, for electricity finally came to Hornby in the late 1930s, and electric lights were also available as extras for a wide range of accessories.

The pride of the Hornby line was a new L.M.S. 4-6-2 Pacific *Princess Elizabeth*, which was first produced in 1937. This was a very large locomotive by anyone's standards, the engine and tender measuring $20\frac{1}{2}$in (52cm), and it came in a special wooden presentation box. In spite of the fact that it was available only as an electric and there was no suitable rolling stock for it, it was enormously popular and sales were surprisingly brisk, considering that it did not fit into the rest of the Hornby system at all and required special wide-radius track to run on. Unfortunately, the die-cast wheels and cast details were prone to metal fatigue, and most of these large locomotives gradually disintegrated inside their nice, wooden carrying cases. Boxed examples in good condition are eagerly collected. The *Princess Elizabeth* was the last, all-new locomotive added to the Hornby gauge O system for on this high point, Hornby ended its development of gauge O tin-plate locomotives.

Hornby L.M.S. *Princess Elizabeth*, 1937 (J)

The final all-new gauge O locomotive to be marketed by Hornby was a giant L.M.S. Pacific: it was to be the company's most ambitious product and a great folly. The effort to produce a scale model was undermined by the ungainly proportions and incorrect details, and, because Hornby had no suitable rolling stock to go with it, the ordinary lithographed L.M.S. coaches were dwarfed by the big Pacific. Plagued by the disintegrating wheel and detail castings, and the lack of suitable track (because the huge and clumsy *Princess Elizabeth* needed special wide-radius steel track in order to run properly), most of these impressive but impractical locomotives rarely left their elaborate wooden display boxes.

Sotheby's, London

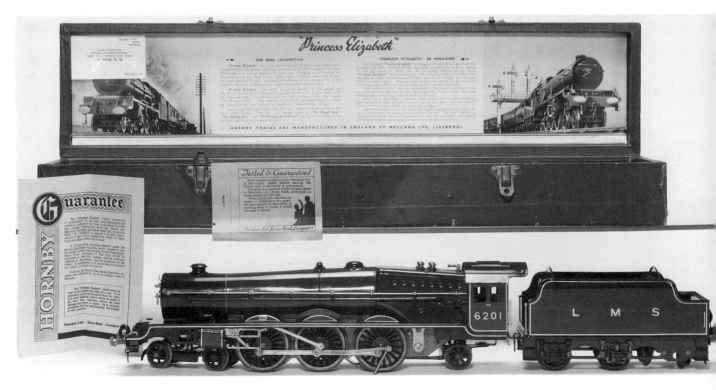

FRENCH PROGRESS

As they were for British manufacturers, the 1930s were golden years for the French toy train industry. J.E.P. became the undisputed leader of the producers of popular gauge O lines. Its lithographed locomotives and coaches were beautifully made, and the firm had managed the difficult task of manufacturing a true 4-6-2 Pacific – one that could also negotiate sharp tin-plate curves. J.E.P.'s Nord *Flèche d'Or* train (*c.*1930), with its wonderfully lithographed Pullmans, was one of the most desirable toy trains ever put on the market. In addition to the fine Pacifics, J.E.P. manufactured a large array of 2-4-0s, 4-4-4s and 4-4-2 streamliners, some steeple-cab electrics and many others. The finish was either lithographed or enamelled steel, and J.E.P. continued to produce a range of gauge O locomotives until the late 1950s.

Rossignol was in decline; although the firm still sold a few cheap trains, its main interest was in clockwork cars and buses, which it continued to manufacture until it went out of business in 1962.

A vigorous new concern had entered the toy train world in the 1930s. L.R., or "Le Rapide", produced an undersized, but smartly styled, range of die-cast gauge O trains, whose weight and extremely low centre of gravity enabled the manufacturers to boast that the firm produced the fastest toy trains in the world. M. Fournereau, who had acquired Marescot's production in 1928, continued to supply the enthusiast market with the Marescot Pacifics and related scale trains.

A rather curious firm, Edobaud, entered the gauge O field in 1931. It produced, exclusively for Galéries Lafayette, a line of giant, electric locomotives and rolling stock in a size that was nearer gauge I than gauge O. The construction methods, which involved screwing all the parts together, were so clumsy and expensive that it is remarkable that the firm managed to stay in business throughout the 1930s.

Also in the 1930s, the French Hornby factory at Bobigny began to expand its range of French outline locomotives. These included an exotic steam outline streamliner and a Bugatti railcar, as well as special French accessories, complete with a very pretty French station.

The Spanish toy industry is one that does not receive the attention it deserves. In the 1930s, the old-established firm of Paya, which had first made clockwork trains in 1918 and electric trains in 1927, made large, lithographed locomotives with rather peculiar wheel arrangements,

Fournereau coaches, 1935 (each coach D)
These French gauge O coaches were designed to accompany the beautiful Etat Pacific, which was originally manufactured by Robert Marescot and continued by Fournereau. Although nicely proportioned and detailed, the Fournereau coaches are rather flimsy, suffer from poor-quality paint and do not usually have interior detail. However, the quality varied enormously, and the examples built from the kits, which were also available, could be either much better or much worse than the built-up versions from the manufacturer. *Sotheby's, London*

mostly 4-4-4s, and some attractive, long, lithographed coaches. A few of these trains were exported, but, apart from Spain, examples of Paya's trains are today found mostly in France.

RENEWED GLORY FOR MÄRKLIN

Märklin, which had regained its strength during the 1920s, enjoyed considerable growth in the 1930s. The growing number of *Reichsbahn* steam outline locomotives produced by the firm was paralleled by an increasing number of very fine electrics, which culminated *c*.1933 in the large, articulated locomotive, the giant Swiss *Crocodile*. This electric locomotive was Märklin's largest and finest, and it was made in gauge I as well as in gauge O. Märklin was the last manufacturer anywhere in the world still manufacturing and improving a gauge I range. As late as 1936 new locomotives and rolling stock were being designed and included in the firm's catalogue. However, some of the new gauge I items had only a short life, for, by 1938, gauge I had been dropped from the catalogue.

In spite of the impressive size of gauge I, by far the most popular and glamorous trains in the 1930s were those made in gauge O. To meet the demand for new gauge O locomotives, Märklin designed a small group of super locomotives, which, the firm hoped, would be the very pinnacle of gauge O refinement. It was a very international collection of prototypes, marking a determined move by Märklin to reintroduce a more international flavour to its range. The new gauge O list included a streamlined 4-6-4 New York Central "Hudson", the *Commodore Vanderbilt* (*c*.1935), as well as an uncatalogued, unstreamlined "Hudson" with matching Pullman coaches. French locomotives were represented by a truly spectacular Etat 4-8-2 *Mountain*, finished either in grey or black. The English locomotive was the experimental, semi-streamlined L.N.E.R. 2-8-4 *Cock o' the North*, available in either green or black. The German *Borsig*, a 4-6-2 Pacific, was a menacing, fully streamlined locomotive painted red, and the giant Swiss *Crocodile* was the final locomotive in the collection.

No other group of locomotives from any other manufacturer can compare with these locomotives. Märklin's 1936 locomotives represented the zenith of the firm's achievements. Today this glamorous group is probably the most expensive series for any collector to complete. The different locomotive types, the size and the variety of colour, coupled with the dashing design and high finish, make this an incomparable series and a triumph for Märklin. Like many another manufacturer, Märklin never equalled this gauge O peak of excellence.

Bing entered the 1930s in unhappy circumstances, and, after releasing a group of entirely new locomotives and rolling stock – some of which were quite good, but not good enough – the firm was wound up in 1933. Some of Bing's equipment was taken over by Karl Bub, which also took Bing's share of the low-priced market, and Bub continued to produce toy trains in the cheap "Nuremberg-style", several of which bore both Bing and Bub trademarks.

Stronlite L.M.S. 2-6-0, 1930 (F); Leeds L.M.S. 4-4-0, 1935 (E); Zeuke *Borsig*, 1950 (E); French Hornby PO, 1946 (C); Stronlite 0-4-0T, 1935 (C); Leeds 0-4-0T, 1925 (D)

Stronlite, an enterprising Japanese company, made occasional attempts to penetrate the British market with good-quality toy trains closely resembling Leeds trains. Although Stronlite's L.M.S. 2-6-0 is not a Leeds wheel arrangement, the styling is very similar to the adjacent Leeds 4-4-0. The Stronlite 0-4-0T industrial tank is an almost exact copy of the Leeds 0-4-0T locomotive, shown here in a very rare livery, which is believed to have been used in stores for advertising Leeds products. The French Hornby electric PO locomotive had a long production life, and it was even manufactured in France under German occupation, with Märklin trademarks added. In spite of the austerities of the post-war recovery in East Germany, the cheerful bakelite *Borsig* locomotive by Zeuke brightened up many a German home. *Courtesy London Toy and Model Museum; S. Willats Collection.*

Märklin Pullman, 1932 (K); Märklin N.Y.C. "Hudson", 1932 (M)

In order to satisfy the demands of Richard Märklin, Märklin's representative in the United States, a small batch of semi-scale "Hudsons" and accompanying scale-length Pullmans was made for sale in the United States. At $50.00 each, the "Hudsons" were not exactly brisk sellers during the Depression years, and the experiment was not followed up. The Pullman cars, painted in a lovely shade of Pullman green, are much more convincing as models than the "Hudson". Their high quality and great rarity ensure a place for these pieces at the top of most Märklin collectors' lists. *Courtesy London Toy and Model Museum*

A newcomer to gauge O manufacture during the 1930s was the old toy company of Fleischmann, which had previously been known for its tin boats and magnetic floating toys. In the late 1930s, however, Fleischmann produced a modest line of cheap, but competently styled, German outline toy trains based on the old Doll trains.

SCALE MODELS BEGIN TO APPEAR

From the time that the first toy train was made, there were pressures to make the trains less like toys and more like the real trains from which they drew their inspiration. From a purely "play" point of view, the ideal configuration was a stubby 0-4-0, running along a wide gauge track and pulling very short, 4-wheeled coaches. A complete gauge I train made in 1900 was shorter than a gauge N train made in 1985 and, therefore, more satisfying as a toy. But, as the 20th century progressed, realism came to be the yardstick against which toy trains were judged. The company that could persuade the public that its trains were the most lifelike had an enormous sales advantage.

All over the world were manufacturers, such as Hornby and Lionel, whose early trains were charming but not necessarily realistic. Initially they could persuade people to buy their products by the force of their advertising and marketing, but eventually they had to make scale trains. Manufacturers were, however, faced by a curious dilemma: the longer and more realistic they made their locomotives and rolling stock, the sillier and less realistic they looked when running on tight, tin-plate curves. Märklin's last, nearly-scale, gauge I trains would have needed a vast area in which to run if they were not to look ridiculous; Lionel's giant Standard gauge trains looked best when they were standing still; and Hornby's *Princess Elizabeth* looked uncomfortable, even when running on the special, wide-radius track.

Märklin's solution to this problem was to reduce the scale. In 1935 the firm developed its gauge OO, which was half the size of gauge O and featured trains scaled at 3.5mm to the foot running on 16.5mm gauge track, a scale and gauge combination that later came to be called HO. By reducing the gauge of the track while retaining a generous radius for the curves, trains of nearly scale proportions looked more realistic when they were running. Moreover, by reducing the size of the trains, manufacturing costs were reduced, and, even though prices were lower, the new scale gave manufacturers a better profit margin.

Several firms had made small gauges before, and even Märklin had experimented with an unsuccessful 26mm gauge in 1912. These previous attempts to sell a miniature gauge had been approached from the wrong angle, however, for the small gauges had been marketed as cheap substitutes for the larger toy trains. In the late 1930s Märklin's new, small gauge trains were marketed as precision scale models; they were even compared to expensive Swiss watches. In spite of the smallness of the trains, Märklin made no compromises with their quality.

The year 1935 saw the launch of another miniature railway system by

Märklin "Jubilee" set, 1935 (M)
In 1935, Märklin celebrated the hundredth anniversary of German railways with a good model, in gauge O, of the first steam train to run on German rails, *Der Adler* (*The Eagle*). This early locomotive was an English "Planet" type 2-2-2 built by Stephenson. The yellow and black coaches were the modified stage-coach designs that were popular in England. Märklin's interpretation is similar in construction to its earlier trains of c.1900, and the soldered assembly and hand-painted details must have given a few old-timers at the Märklin plant a rare chance to exercise their skills. *Phillips*

Märklin HS 65/13021 Swiss electric, 1932 (M); Märklin 42cm Mitropa coach, 1932 (H); Pair of Märklin 40cm radial roof coaches, 1930 (each coach (H)
The large Swiss electric, in gauge I, was Märklin's top-of-the-line electric outline locomotive during the early 1930s. Usually brown, the version shown here is in the very rare green livery with a white roof. The 42cm (1ft 4½in) coach series were the short-lived successors to the popular 40cm (1ft 3¾in) P.L.M.-type coaches, which had originally been introduced in 1912. To up-date these old coaches for their last year of manufacture, the normal clerestory roofs were replaced by more modern radial roofs. *Phillips*

Trix, a new German company founded by Stefan Bing, who had left Gebrüder Bing in 1927 to take over the Nuremberg firm of Förtner & Haffner, which made tin-plate toys. The Trix system used the same gauge as Märklin – 16.5mm – but it was a slightly smaller scale, 1:90 as opposed to 1:87. The reduced scale was a better match for the gauge than the old Bing "table-top" railway scale of 1:76. Trix Express, later better known in England as Trix Twin, was not as realistic as Märklin's system, and the wheels and track were more coarsely made. However, it was interesting electrically and had the ability to run two trains at the same time on the same track, a feature that definitely had more "play value". The Trix system, which had German outline trains, was slightly modified for its simultaneous introduction into Britain through Bassett-Lowke. In 1938, when the firm's directors were replaced by men favoured by the Nazi party, Stefan Bing and his associates moved to Britain and established a separate factory to handle the British trade. Like everything else sold by Bassett-Lowke, British Trix was expensive. Unfortunately, compared with Märklin's small gauge system, it was rather toy-like.

Hornby had been watching the development of small gauge railways with some interest and, in 1938, launched its own system. As a system, it was closer in concept to Märklin than to Trix, for Hornby's intention was to provide a miniature railway system that would appeal to the scale model enthusiast rather than to produce an intriguing toy train with "play value" as Trix had done. The locomotives and rolling stock were, therefore, much more convincing as scale models. Like Märklin, Hornby called its new system "OO", but unfortunately it chose the old Bing table-top scale of 1:76, a mis-match between scale and gauge that has plagued British modellers for over 50 years. However, since British prototypes are built to a much smaller loading gauge than anything on the continent or in the United States, the resulting models did not look significantly out of scale.

AMERICAN SMALL GAUGES

Flushed with the success of its gauge O "Hudson", Lionel introduced a small gauge system of its own in 1938–9. The scale O 4-6-4 "Hudson" was reduced to 1:76 size, and a handful of die-cast freight cars, copied from the designs of a company called Scalecraft, which specialized in

Lionel *Flying Yankee* set, 1935 (G); Lionel 252 set, 1932 (D)
Only three years separate these two small gauge O sets in the Lionel catalogue, but there is a world of difference in the styling and constructional details. The *Flying Yankee* is pure "American" in concept and execution and, although small, exudes a feeling of power and speed. The 252 set, on the other hand, is a "cute" toy train (painted in bright orange) from the 1920s. Both sets are very collectable, but the 252 set wins on charm – and has the additional advantage of being cheaper. *Sotheby's, New York*

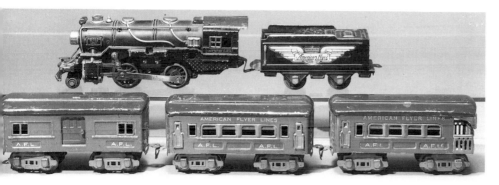

American Flyer 2-4-0 train set, 1931 (D)
Electric drive and a working headlamp are features of this gauge O set from the Depression. The die-castings used in the locomotive's construction were still decorated with copper domes, chimneys, pipes, pumps and other details, similar to the style that had characterized Lionel trains in the 1920s and early 1930s. The neat 8-wheeled coaches have plenty of brass trim, including axle boxes. American Flyer is an interesting company and it produced a wide range of trains, which are still undervalued; a large collection may be assembled for only moderate cost.
Sotheby's, New York

scale models, completed the train. To match the scale, a track gauge of 19mm was chosen, and this combination of scale and gauge was called "OO" by Lionel and other American manufacturers of scale models, including Scalecraft and Nason. (The modern British equivalent is called EM gauge.) The Lionel OO system suffered from corporate neglect and was not developed beyond the initial launch, disappearing from the company's range during World War II, never to be revived. Just why Lionel introduced gauge OO is not clear, but it must have been part of its flirtation with scale model railroading at the end of the 1930s. The interesting experiment was, sadly, short-lived, but as models, the Lionel OO trains were among the best produced by any company anywhere.

Under A.C. Gilbert's management the revived American Flyer company also brought out a small gauge, or "HO" gauge, railway, which had rails 16.5mm apart and a scale of 1:87. This attractive, die-cast railway had the usual 4-6-4 "Hudson" and a rake of die-cast passenger coaches, as well as freight cars. The American Flyer HO system was more extensive than Lionel's OO system and looked very promising.*

Alone among the French manufacturers, J.E.P. was in the process of bringing out an HO system, but the war intervened and the system was shelved until the late 1940s.

The outbreak of World War II put an end to many manufacturers' plans and hopes. Neither American Flyer nor Lionel revived its small gauge trains after the war, during which, like many American companies, they turned their factories over to war production. In Germany, Märklin was taken over for the manufacture of munitions, Karl Bub's factory was bombed several times, and the Nuremberg factories of both Trix and Günthermann were destroyed. Lehmann, exceptionally, managed to continue production, selling to neutral countries. British factories, too, were put over to war work, toy train production at Hornby, for example, not restarting until 1947.

Although the 1930s ended with a glorious burst of gauge O activity, it really marked the end of gauge O as a viable toy train system. The future lay with the emerging small-scale model railway systems that were eventually to eliminate the traditional toy train altogether.

* Unlike Lionel's OO gauge, the Gilbert HO range had a post-war life. Although five different locomotives were available, it was not especially popular with the scale-minded model railroaders.

7

THE DEMISE OF THE TOY TRAIN 1945–55

The end of World War II found almost all of the toy train companies intact and prepared to put their pre-war lines back on the market. Europe had been hit hard by the war, and austerity and the widespread shortages of raw materials meant that recovery was slow for firms like Hornby and Märklin. New firms had started up, particularly in Switzerland and Italy, but it was in the United States that toy train makers like Lionel and American Flyer were in the best position to resume full-scale production.

American Flyer had the advantage of having in stock a line that had been completely redesigned in 1938–40. Although the size was smaller than the normal gauge O 1:43 scale, the proportions and detail of the trains were excellent. After the war, American Flyer reduced the distance between the tracks to 24mm, so that the gauge was a better match for the scale, and it christened the result "S" gauge. American Flyer's HO trains were not revived, and the firm concentrated all its effort into producing the new "S" gauge trains.

Lionel was even quicker off the mark than American Flyer, and it soon had a sizeable catalogue of new trains, all of which made extensive use of pressure die-castings. The old tin-plate look had vanished, as had the streamliners from the Depression years. Like American Flyer, Lionel concentrated on semi-scale gauge O trains and dropped its scale model efforts, such as the pre-war "Hudson" and the gauge OO sets.

BOOM YEARS FOR AMERICA

America was enjoying a post-war boom, and Lionel did not see any need to diversify its product line. The huge pent-up demand from buyers who had been unable to afford toy trains during the Depression of the 1930s

Lionel 6-8-8 steam turbine, 1946 (D); Lionel 6457 caboose, 1951 (A); Lionel A.T.S.F. 3464X box car, 1950 (A)
One of the first locomotives to be produced by Lionel after World War II, the Pennsylvania steam turbine has the distinction of being the toy locomotive with the greatest number of wheels – 20 or, if the tender is included, 32. To achieve this technical truimph, Lionel had to select a prototype with no awkward steam cylinders that would get in the way; to reduce the size rather drastically; and to substitute some undersized flangeless rollers for the centre wheels in the leading and trailing trucks. The locomotive is almost completely made of heavy metal die-castings, but the caboose and box car are of much lighter plastic castings. The box car has a small plunger, which, when moved, opens the door and moves the man inside. *Phillips*

and had been frustrated by the lack of production during the war meant that Lionel did not have to hunt for customers. A new programme was begun that emphasized automatic accessories and electrical novelties; almost all the new accessories "did" something. Most popular was a refrigerator car: a man inside unloaded miniature milk churns on to a loading platform when a button was pushed. Lionel also produced ore-dumping cars, conveyor belts to load coal, saw mills, barrel loaders, log loaders, oil derricks that bubbled and a water tower that appeared to pump water. The new accessories were ingenious but not very realistic, and, while popular with children, their toy-like qualities did not please serious buyers who wanted to build realistic railways.

The new Lionel locomotives were an impressive lot, and even though the large 6-8-6 Pennsylvania steam turbine was severely undersized, it did have 20 wheels, which was more than any other toy locomotive. Lionel trains puffed smoke, whistled, had magnetically enhanced traction and everything on the railway had electric lights. The new, very nearly full-scale sized freight and passenger diesel locomotives were not only colourful but also very convincing models. The most glamorous post-war Lionel locomotive was the streamlined Pennsylvania GG1, a sleek and heavy 4-6-6-4 electric locomotive with the same refined but aggressive good looks that characterized the prototype design by Raymond Lowey.

For 10 years Lionel and American Flyer enjoyed record sales and ignored the developments that were taking place outside their own closed worlds. But people everywhere were becoming much more interested in scale model railroading and, by the mid-1950s, ready-to-run HO train sets had become cheap and widely available. The post-war toy train boom was suddenly over, and the sharp decline in the sales of the relatively expensive gauge O trains caught both Lionel and American Flyer unprepared. Desperate remedies were tried, but both companies went under. American Flyer stopped production, and Lionel trains became a small, loss-making subsidiary of a large conglomerate. The long era of American toy train manufacturing was effectively over.

AUSTERITY IN BRITAIN

In Britain, Bassett-Lowke and Hornby both had plans to re-activate their pre-war gauge O trains while, at the same time, expanding their OO/HO systems. For both firms small gauges took priority, and their increasing popularity delayed the gauge O schedule to such an extent that Hornby's post-war gauge O locomotives never progressed beyond a few different 0-4-0s and some 4-wheeled passenger coaches, although the 8-wheeled coaches were available for a short time. Hornby's scarce resources were largely allocated to the manufacturing of the much more profitable Hornby Dublo (the company's registered name for its gauge OO items), and the once-proud gauge O system died a lingering death in the mid-1950s.

Meanwhile, Winteringham, now renamed Precision Scale Models,

J.E.P. *Mistral*, 1965 (G); Lionel
Pennsylvania GGI, 1955 (E); French
Hornby TNB, 1961 (E); French Hornby
OBB, 1959 (F); French Hornby TZB,
1961 (E)
The post-war years favoured electric
outline locomotives, and some of the
best were made in France. The

magnificent die-cast *Mistral* was the
swan song of the famous French firm
J.E.P. (Jouets de Paris), which had been
manufacturing gauge O locomotives
from the turn of the century. The TNB
and TZB were also die-cast and were
the finest, but also the last, locomotives
to be marketed by French Hornby. The

sturdy Lionel GGI, which has a similar
die-cast construction, does not look out
of place in such company, but the OBB's
tin-plate construction is more typical of
the designs that were popular in the
1930s. *S. Willats Collection*

was struggling to produce both the gauge O line for Bassett-Lowke and the HO line for Trix. The sales of the rather drab and lifeless gauge O trains were sluggish and were not helped by the astronomical prices asked for the better locomotives. Consequently, sales of the expensive trains shrank to the point where one man, Vic Hunt, who had been commissioned by Bassett-Lowke after the war to build its more expensive and detailed models, was capable of making sufficient high-quality locomotives to fill any demand. Precision Scale Models itself was dragged under by faltering sales of the out-moded Trix trains, which were not only less realistic but also more expensive than any other small gauge system. The liquidation of Precision Scale Models in the late 1950s meant the end of Bassett-Lowke's range of semi-mass-produced gauge O trains. W.J. Bassett-Lowke died in 1953; the company's model train production declined, and its retail outlet was reduced to a dim and dusty curiosity, supplying a few bits to a steadily shrinking band of loyal customers, while the main firm concentrated on industrial models and museum pieces.

Other specialist gauge O manufacturers survived into the bleak post-war years in Britain. Exley, the Bradford-based firm, accepted orders to build passenger coaches, along with occasional wagons and locomotives based on L.M.S. designs. Mills Brothers of Sheffield (Milbro), like Exley, undertook special commissions, and the firm produced expensive, hand-made rolling stock as well as a small series of fine-scale gauge O locomotives; the firm was, perhaps, best known, however, for its rather curious teak-finish L.N.E.R. coaches. Also continuing to produce gauge O items was the Leeds Model Co., which had made its name with a range of wooden-bodied Pullman coaches, decorated with stuck-on litho-

Bassett-Lowke B.R. *Flying Scotsman*, 1950 (l)

The *Flying Scotsman* in British Railways livery was the final version of a very handsome and popular gauge O Bassett-Lowke locomotive. Although finely proportioned and relatively expensive, the *Flying Scotsman* was a lithographed locomotive, a method of manufacture usually associated with the cheaper end of the market. Since lithographed finished and tabbed construction were the hallmarks of the Nuremberg style, the Bassett-Lowke Pacific could be considered the highest expression of that style. The *Flying Scotsman* was the most popular of the expensive Bassett-Lowke locomotives, and it was available with either clockwork or electric drive, both of which were very good mechanisms. *Phillips*

graphed paper. Although not built to scale, Leeds gauge O locomotives were attractive; but the frames and wheels, made of a zinc alloy, were unfortunately prone to metal fatigue. Leeds was also the first toy train manufacturer to use bakelite for both passenger coaches and wagons. None of these companies, however, was ever to revive the interest in gauge O that had existed before the war, and they gradually dwindled into obscurity, unable to compete with the new mass-produced small gauge models.

GAUGE O IN FRANCE

In France after the war gauge O proved to be more popular than in Britain, and the three major suppliers – J.E.P., French Hornby and L.R. – enjoyed considerable success for several years. Like Lionel, J.E.P. had switched to die-casting to manufacture trains and was producing France's finest range of gauge O equipment. The most popular items in the J.E.P. range were a beautiful 12-wheeled Mistral electric locomotive and a magnificent P.L.M. 2-8-2 steam type with two motors.

By the end of the 1950s, J.E.P. sales had begun to fall and the firm tried to market a stop-gap "S" gauge system. Sadly, it was a total flop. The early 1960s saw J.E.P.'s final efforts to remain in business, but the new HO system that was produced was too late to save the famous company, and, in 1965, its factory was closed down.

French Hornby had produced an improved post-war gauge O catalogue, which was, in every respect, superior to British Hornby, for it contained a good selection of gauge O locomotives and accessories. Eventually, French Hornby had to drop its charming gauge O trains in favour of HO, but it was still unable to meet the competition and, like J.E.P., vanished from the French scene in the 1960s.

The third major French company to survive into the post-war period was L.R. (Louis Roussy), whose "Le Rapide", super-fast trains had sold so well in the late 1930s (see page 137). L.R. trains were small in relation to their gauge, which gave them greater realism when running and so added greatly to their appeal. However, when commercial HO became popular, the L.R. compromise of scale and gauge looked less attractive, and L.R. stopped production in 1954.

The Spanish company of Paya had been making gauge O since the 1920s, and by the 1960s, it was the last company anywhere still manufacturing gauge O toy trains. The pride of the line was an impressive 2-6-2 "Santa Fé" steam locomotive. The engine was made with good detail, and it had an unusual 8-wheeled tender and as well as a mechanism that puffed smoke. Large 8-wheeled tin-plate coaches complemented this attractive engine, which was close to Märklin in style. Unfortunately the die-castings, used extensively for detail, and motor parts, were prone to metal fatigue, and most surviving "Santa Fé's" are non-runners.

During the war, a small toy train industry had started in Switzerland, which had, until shortly before World War II, always been well supplied

OPPOSITE ABOVE **Biaggi Italian electric, 1947 (E); Sakai 2-6-0, 1947(?) (E); Moskabel diesel, 1964 (E); Buco Swiss electric, 1945 (E); J.E.P. railcar, 1935 (F)** The variety of toy trains made for gauge O is probably greater than the total made for all the other gauges. This illustration brings together a diverse group of gauge O trains representing several countries. The Italian electric by Biaggi is a little known gauge O effort by a manufacturer better known for gauge I. The Japanese steam type was probably made both before and after World War II, and although the heavy, Lionel-styled locomotive looks American in inspiration, it is probably based on a Japanese prototype. Note that the couplers are copies of the Märklin "fix" coupler. The Russian diesel is a rugged giant, which dwarfs the finely made but uninspired Swiss electric. Finally, the huge French railcar by J.E.P. would not disgrace a gauge I layout. This monster was in production until the mid-1950s, and good examples are not hard to find. *Courtesy London Toy and Model Museum*

OPPOSITE BELOW **Biaggi Etat *Mountain* 4-8-2, 1955 (H)** The gauge I Etat *Mountain* by Biaggi was one of a series of limited editions of fine locomotives manufactured during the post-war years by this small Italian manufacturer. Almost hand built, these locomotives echo the Märklin tradition in their finish and detailing. *Courtesy London Toy and Model Museum*

by German manufacturers, particularly Märklin. In the absence of German manufacturers, however, a small native industry was established. Cheap gauge O trains were supplied between 1944 and the mid-1950s by Buco, which produced a range of Swiss outline locomotives, while larger engines were made by Keiser and by Hag (H.A. Gahler).

By the end of the 1950s, most companies had stopped manufacturing gauge O toy trains or had switched to making limited-run, scale models. Various other obscure toy trains, usually gauge O, were produced in the post-war years by small firms such as Zeuke of East Germany, Loma Wein of Austria and Merkur of Czechoslovakia. Small companies in Poland, Russia, Hungary and Belgium manufactured limited quantities of toy trains primarily for local markets, but it is difficult to assess the output of these companies because very few catalogues have come to light.

In Japan, at least two toy train companies that had sold gauge O trains during the 1930s continued to do so after the war. Japan's best-known firm was Stronlite, which made good copies of Leeds equipment: Stronlite Pullmans were, in fact, better than those produced by Leeds. Sakai, the other main Japanese company, made a range of Japanese outline steam and electric locomotives and rolling stock, which was a curious blend of Lionel and Märklin features. All their equipment, which was electrically powered, was very heavy.

ITALIAN ENTERPRISE

Surprisingly, in Italy, a country that had not been prominent in the pre-war production of toy trains, several toy train firms sprang up, although most survived for only a short time. Two companies, however, Biaggi and Elettren, were successful in opening up a new market for high-quality toy trains for the enthusiast collector. Both companies produced limited runs of top-quality, expensive toy trains and both companies are still in existence today. Biaggi primarily made locomotives in gauges O and I as well as small amounts of rolling stock. Produced in small batches, Biaggi locomotives were similar in size and style to those offered by Märklin before the war.

Elettren made only two locomotives, concentrating instead on a very fine line of passenger coaches with elaborate interior detail. The two Elettren locomotives followed Italian prototypes, and they were made to a larger size than the normal scale O. One was a big, handsome, Italian, electric type, with 16 wheels. The other was a super-detailed Italian F.S. 4-6-2 Pacific. Unfortunately, both locomotives were prone to metal fatigue from faulty die-castings. The Elettren coaches, also built to a larger-than-normal scale, were more successful, and they were, and still are, the best passenger coaches ever produced by any toy train manufacturer. They are still being produced and are today sold through the Swiss firm of Fulgurex. Both the locomotives and the coaches produced by Elettren represent an effort to continue and improve upon the pre-war trains produced by Märklin.

Elettren Italian State Railways 4-4-4-4 electric, 1950 (H)
The Italian firm of Elettren had originally planned to produce a comprehensive range of top quality gauge O trains for the post-war market. These trains were intended to surpass anything that had gone before in terms of super-detailing and quality construction. Two locomotives were made: an Italian steam outline Pacific and the magnificent 4-4-4-4 electric, which could be bought with one or two motors. The boldness of the casting detail contributed to the undoubted "eye appeal" of the classic heavy Italian electric. Impurities in the metal mix caused the castings to disintegrate over a period of time and few have survived intact. *Sotheby's, London*

POST-WAR GERMANY

In Germany, Fleischmann, which had taken over Doll in 1938, made a few of its pre-war type gauge O trains before changing over to the production of high-quality HO scale models. The firm is now very active, producing attractive and beautifully made scale model trains. Karl Bub was not so lucky: the last surviving old Nuremberger sank almost all of its available capital into a new "S" gauge system, which failed to sell. This disaster fatally crippled Bub, which staggered on, making a few, very cheap, gauge O trains before stopping production altogether in 1966.

Märklin, which had developed an extensive HO system before the war, was in a strong position in the post-war market. Like Hornby, Märklin revived a small proportion of its extensive pre-war range, even going so far as to put the German 4-6-2 Pacific back into production. Nothing new was added to the gauge O range, however, and in the 1950s the company finally stopped producing gauge O items altogether. It was obvious to Märklin that HO gauge was the key to success – the company had, after all, seen that trend as early as 1936 – and by the mid-1950s, Märklin was the sole survivor of the early German toy-train companies.

The era of the toy train had lasted for over a hundred years, and during that time the concept of the toy train had gone through many phases. A common thread running throughout the entire period was the constant search for greater realism. Some marvellous compromises were produced – trains that satisfied the enthusiast as well as the child – but, in the end, the scale models won and the children lost. The cheerful, brightly coloured, imaginative and rugged toy train has been transformed into the technically perfect, cold and delicate, scale model that would never run on any child's dream railway. Now all the train buyers are adults, and children are no longer interested in finding trains under the Christmas tree.

INTERNATIONAL INDEX OF MANUFACTURERS

Argentina
Duvaz
Matarazzo

Australia
Austral
Ferris
Fox
Maulyn
Robilt

Austria
Ditmar
Liliput
Löma Wien

Belgium
C.A.M.

Brazil
Atma
Frateschi
Metalma

Chile
Doggenweiler

Croatia
Mehanotecnika

Czech Republic
Ets
Lastra
Merkur
Minor
Sebella
Tioka
Zbrojevnka

Denmark
D.F.D.S.
Long
Pioner-Expressen
Wittrock

France
Antal
A.S.
Ateco
Bascou
B.L.Z.
Brianne
Chaumeil
C.R. (Charles Rossignol)
D.S. (Dessin)
Edobaud
Effel
Fex-Miniatrain
Fournereau/Marescot
France-Trains
F.V. (Emile Favre)
G.E.M.
Gerard-Tab
Heller & Coudray
Hornby (France)
J.C. (J. Caron)
J.E.P. (Jouets de Paris)
Jouef
Joustra
Jucsie

L.G.
L.R. (Le Rapide)
Maltête & Parent
Martin
G.P. (Georges Parent)
PMP (P.M. Pillon)
Punch
Radiguet & Massiot
R.M.A.
Rateau
S.I.F. (Société Industrielle de Ferblanterie)
S.M.C.F.
V.B.

Germany
Arnold
Beckh
Ottmar Bekh
Berlinerbahn
Biller
Bing
Karl Bub
Buchner
Carette
Distler
Doll
Eggerbahn
Einfalt
Falk
Fischer
Fleischmann
Günthermann
Gutzold
Hamo
Emil Hausmann
Hehr
Heinzl
Mathias Hess/J.L. Hess
Issmayer
Keim
Kibri
J. Kraus/Fandor
L.B.Z.
Lehmann
Liebmann
Löhmann
Lutz
Märklin
Merker & Fischer
Pico
Plank
Rock & Graner (R. &G.N)
Rokal
Schönner
Schnabel
Paul Schreiber
Paul Schroeder, Berlin
A.S. Schumann
Gottfried Striebel
Stadtilm
Trix-Twin, Trix Express
HeinrichWimmer(H.W.N.)

Zeuke

Great Britain
Betal
Bar Knight
Bassett-Lowke Ltd
J. Bateman & Co.
Birmingham Engineering Co. ("Tessted" Toys)
Bowman
Brimtoy
W. Britain & Son
Burnett
British Flyer (American Flyer)
British Modelling & Electric Co.
Carson
Chad Valley
Clyde Model Dockyard
Electro Model
Eveready
Exley
Graham Farish
Hornby
Jones & Co.
Jubb
Leeds Model Co./Stedman
Lines
Lone Star
Lucas & Davies
Mamod
Marx
Mettoy
Milbro
Mills, W.
Newton & Co
Parks, R.W.
Primus
Shaw & Co.
Steven's Model Dockyard
John Theobald & Co.
Toby-Baxtoy
Triang
Trix
Walker-Fenn
Wallworks
Wells Brimtoy
Whiles, H.
Whitanco
Whitney
Winteringham/Precision-Scale Models
Wood, H.J.
Wrenn

Italy
Biaggi
Bral
Camsa
Conti
Elettren
G.E.M.
Gisea

Inco
Ingap
Lima
Pocher
Rivarossi
Roco

Japan
Akane
Alpha
Aster
Bandai
Cragstan
K.T.M.
New One
Rosco
Sakai/Seki
Stronlite
Tenshodo

Korea
Samhongsa

Spain
Electrotrain
Garvi
Ibertren
Josfel
Manamo
Mataro
Paya
Rico
Treco
Valtoy

Russia
Moskabel

Switzerland
Albrecht
Blum-Flos
Buco
Car-Jibby
Darstaed
Erno
Fulgurex
Junior
Hag
Keiser
Leuthold
Löwenstein
Matha
Metropolitan
Milodor
Minia
Resal
Spiewa
Wesa
Wilag

United States
A.H.M.
Althof Bergmann & Co
American Display Co.
American Flyer/Gilbert
American Miniature Railway Co.
Arcade

Aristocraft
Athearn
Beggs, Eugene
Bliss, R.
Bowser
Boucher
George W. Brown & Co.
Buddy "L"
Carlisle & Finch
Carpenter, Francis
Carrollton Novelty Co.
Central Loco. Works
Dayton
Dent
Dorfan
Elektoy
Fallows (IXL)
Francis, Field & Francis
Garlick
Girard Model Works
Grey Iron Casting
Hafner/Wyandotte
Harris Toy Company
Hoge
Howard
Hubley
Hull & Stafford
Ives
Icken
Katz
Ken Kidder
Kenton Hardware Co.
Knapp Electric & Novelty Co.
Lionel
Lobaugh
Mantua-Tyco
Mechanicraft
Marx Corporation
Mettoy
Milton Bradley
Pratt & Letchworth
Parmele & Sturgis
Penn Line
Railcraft
Richart
Roundhouse
Reed
Saginaw
Scale Craft
Secor
Schrader
Suydam
Wm. Shimer & Son
J. & E. Stevens
Stevens & Brown Mfing Co.
Union Manufacturing Co.
Voltamp Electric Mfing Co.
Weeden
Wilkins

TOY TRAIN GAUGES

In the early days of toy railways, the gauge, or track width, was measured from rail centre to rail centre. There were problems with this method, and eventually a more accurate system was adopted that measured the distance between the inside edge of each rail. For the larger gauges, the new measurement was usually 2–3mm narrower than the old one. Gauge I was 48mm between the rails using the old standard; 45mm using the new standard. Fine scale modellers had problems because scale is related to gauge, but toy train manufacturers' standards for scale were much more flexible, and there were large variations in the scales of the toy trains running on each gauge.

There were some interesting coincidences. American 2in gauge was 51mm from rail centre to rail centre, but thin, strip rails, set on edge, were used by all manufacturers of 2in gauge equipment, which meant that the 51mm measurement was also the distance between the inside edges of the rails. European gauge II was 54mm from rail centre to rail centre, but only 51mm, measured from the inside edges. Gauge II and 2in gauge were, therefore, compatible. For the same reason, Lionel $2\frac{7}{8}$in gauge was compatible with the European 75mm gauge III/IV.

For several years European manufacturers labelled anything smaller that gauge O as gauge OO.

All this confusion is reflected in the table. The gauges and names shown are the ones used by the manufacturers in their advertising and catalogues. They are more useful for identification than accurate measurements.

Major manufacturers	16.5	18	19	24	25	26	28	30	35	48	51	54	57	65	67	73	75	85	90	115	12
American Flyer	HO			S					O				W								
Bassett-Lowke	HO/OO								O	I		II			III		IV				
Biaggi									O	I											
Bing	OO				OO		OO		O	I		II	U		III		IV				
Bub	OO			S/OO					O	I											
Carette				U	OO		OO	U	O	I		II		III	III						
Carlisle & Finch											2in										
Distler	U						OO		O												
Dorfan									O				W								
Gamages	OO				1in		$1\frac{1}{8}$in		O	I		II			$2\frac{1}{2}$in		III				
Hornby	OO								O												
Issmayer					U		U	U	O	I											
Ives									O	I			W								
J.E.P.		U		S			U		O												
Lionel			OO						O				ST				$2\frac{7}{8}$in				
Märklin	OO/HO					OO			O	I		II	U				III				U
Plank									O	I				VIII							
Schönner					OOO		OO		O	I		II			IIA		III	IV	U	U	
Trix	OO																				
Voltamp											2in										

U = Unnamed   W = Wide gauge   ST = Standard gauge

GLOSSARY

American outline: the phrase used to describe a locomotive that has typically American features: a tall smokestack (qv), a large headlamp, a bell and no splashers (qv).

Atlantic: a locomotive with a 4–4–2 wheel configuration.

bi-polar: a type of electric locomotive popularized by the Minneapolis and St Paul Railroad in the 1920s and used as a prototype by all the U.S. toy train manufacturers.

bogie: a low truck running on one or more pairs of wheels; it is attached in front of or behind the locomotive's driving wheels or to the ends of a long railway carriage by a pivot on which it swivels freely on bends.

British outline: the phrase used to describe a locomotive that has typically British features: a smallish cab, a low funnel or chimney, splashers (qv) and a whistle.

"Bury": an early locomotive, so called from the name of its manufacturer; the wheel configuration is usually 0–4–0.

caboose: the American name for the guard's van; a car on a goods train for workmen.

clerestory: the raised section of a carriage roof with windows or ventilators.

coupe vent: see wind-splitter.

cowcatcher: a metal structure situated at the front of American locomotives to clear obstacles from the track; also known as a pilot.

die-casting: a casting from a metal mould made under high pressure.

"dribbler" or **"piddler"**: a steam-propelled, spirit-fired locomotive, which tended to leave a trail of water from the cylinder behind it.

electric outline: the phrase used to describe a locomotive that looks as if it runs on electricity but that may, in fact, be clockwork.

floor-runner: a push-pull or carpet train that had no motive power but was propelled by hand.

German outline: the phrase used to describe a locomotive that has typically German features: usually a large cab and sometimes splashers (qv).

inter-urban: the American term for a tram that resembles a streetcar and that runs on rails between cities.

journal: the part of a shaft or axle that rests on bearings.

journal box: an oil box containing the grease used to lubricate the ends of the axles.

Norris-type: an early locomotive, manufactured by the Norris Locomotive Works in the United States; the locomotive featured a high-domed fire box and a leading bogie. Locomotives of this type were widely exported to other countries.

Pacific: a locomotive with a 4–6–2 wheel configuration.

pantograph: a diamond-shaped structure situated above a locomotive or carriage that collects electric current from overhead wires.

permanent magnet motors: motors in which the magnet is able to operate with or without electricity.

"Planets": the first British locomotives; named after different planets, such as *Mars*, they had a characteristic 2–2–2 wheel configuration.

rake: a group of coaches, coupled to a locomotive, which makes up a train.

scale outline: the phrase used to describe a scale model as distinct from a toy train.

Single: a type of locomotive with only one pair of driving wheels.

six-coupled: a locomotive that has six driving wheels.

skating coupling rod: a special connecting rod with slots that, when the rod is fastened on to a locomotive's driving wheels, permit the wheels to revolve independently of each other.

smokestack: the American term for the chimney, or funnel, of a locomotive.

spectacle plate: a vertical steel plate found on early locomotives that had no cabs; the plate, which provided protection against the weather, had two round windows resembling spectacles.

splasher: a wheel-cover that prevents mud being thrown up against the engine and protects passengers standing in stations; a mudguard.

steam outline: the phrase used to describe a locomotive that looks as if it were propelled by steam, although it might, in fact, be driven by electricity or clockwork.

steeple cab: a cab with a high (or steeple-like) central portion of its upper part.

Storkleg: a configuration with 2 small and 2 large driving wheels, which, some thought, resembled a stork standing on one leg.

tender: a wagon carrying coal and water, pulled behind a locomotive.

truck: the North American term for a bogie.

wind-splitter: an early streamlined style typical of German and French locomotives; it was characterized by V-shaped chimneys, domes, cab and boiler front. Locomotives in this style were also called *coupe vents*.

BIBLIOGRAPHY

Adams, J.H.L. and Whitehouse, P.B., *Model and Miniature Railways*, Hamlyn/New English Library, London, 1976

Alexander, Edwin P., *The Collector's Book of the Locomotive*, Clarkson N. Potter, Inc., New York, 1966

Ayres, William S., *The Warner Collector's Guide to American Toys*, The Main Street Press, Warner Books Inc., New York, 1981

Baecker, Carlernst and Väterlein, Christian, *Vergessenes Blechspielzeug (Germany's Forgotten Toymakers)*, Frankfurter Fachbuchhandlung Michael Kohl, Frankfurt am Main, 1982

Baecker, Carlernst and Wagner, Botho G., *Blechspielzeug Eisenbahnen*, Battenberg Verlag, Munich, 1982

Barenholtz, Bernard and McClintock, Ingz, *American Antique Toys*, New Cavendish Books, London, 1980

Bartholomew, Charles, *Mechanical Toys*, Hamlyn Publishing Group, Feltham, Middlesex, 1979

Bassett-Lowke, W.J., *Model Railways volumes I and II*, W.J. Bassett-Lowke & Co., Northampton, 1906–8

Bassett-Lowke, W.J., *The Model Railway Handbook volumes III–XV*, W.J. Bassett-Lowke & Co., Northampton, 1910–50

Becher, Udo, *Auf Kleinen Spuren*, Transpress, Berlin, 1970

—, *Early Tinplate Model Railways*, V.E.B. Verlag für Verkehrswesen, 1979; Argus Books, Hemel Hempstead, Hertfordshire, 1980

Becher, Udo and Reiche, Werner, *Bodenläufer Spielbahn Supermodell*, Durchgesehene Lizenzausgabe der Alba Buchverlag GmbH & Co. K.G., Dusseldorf/Editions Leipzig, 1981

Brauch, Margot and Bangert, Albrecht, *Jouets Mécaniques Anciens*, Plenary Publications, 1980; L'Editions Duculot, Paris-Gembloux, 1981

Carstens, Harold H., *The Trains of Lionel's Standard Gauge Era*, Railroad Model Craftsman, 1964

Cieslik, Jürgen, *Blech Spielzeug*, Wilhelm Heyne Verlag, Munich, 1980

Cieslik, Jürgen, Jorgens, Dorothee, Miller, Monika and Väterlein, Christian; Münchner Stadtmuseum; *Die Welt aus Blech*, Philipp von Zabern, Mainz am Rhein, 1981

Cieslik, Jürgen and Marianne, *Lehmann Toys*, New Cavendish Books, London, 1982

Coluzzi, Count Giansanti, *The Trains on Avenue de Rumine*, New Cavendish Books/Editions Serge Godin, 1982

Corredor-Matheos, J., *La Joguina a Catalunya*, Edicions 62, S.A., Barcelona, 1981

Ellis, Hamilton, *Model Railways 1838–1939*, Allen & Unwin, London, 1962

Foster, Michael, *Hornby Dublo Trains*, New Cavendish Books, London, 1980

Fraley, Donald S., *Lionel Trains, Standard of the World 1900–1943*, Train Collectors' Association, 1976

Fritzsch, Karl Ewald and Bachman, Manfred, *An Illustrated History of Toys*, Editions Leipzig, 1965; Abbey Library, 1966

Fuller, Roland *The Bassett-Lowke Story*, New Cavendish Books, London, 1984

Gardiner, Gordon and Morris, Alistair, *The Price Guide to Metal Toys*, Antique Collectors' Club, Woodbridge, Suffolk, 1980

—, *Metal Toys*, Salamander Books, London, 1984

Godel, Howard, *Antique Toy Trains*, Exposition Press Inc., Smithtown, N.Y., 1976

Gomm, P.G., *Older Locomotives 1900–1942*, Thomas Nelson, Walton-on-Thames, 1970

Graebe, Chris and Julie, *The Hornby Gauge O System*, New Cavendish Books, London, 1985

Greenberg, Bruce C., *Greenberg's Price Guide to Lionel Trains, 0 and 0–27 Trains 1945–1977*, Greenberg Publishing Co., Sykesville, Maryland, 1977

—, *Greenberg's Price Guide to Lionel Trains 1901–1942*, Greenberg Publishing Co., Sykesville, Maryland, 1979

Hare, Frank C., Burke, James J., Jr. and Wolken, I. Stephen, *Toy Train Treasury, volume I*, Iron Horse Productions, 1974

—, *Toy Train Treasury volume II*, Iron Horse Productions, 1974

Harley, Basil, *Toyshop Steam*, Model and Allied Publications, Argus Books, Hemel Hempstead, Hertfordshire, 1978

Hertz, Louis H., *Riding the Tinplate Rails*, Model Craftsman Publishing Co., 1944

—, *Messrs Ives of Bridgeport*, Mark Haber & Co., 1950

—, *New Roads to Adventure in Model Railroading*, Simmons-Boardman Publishing Co., 1952

—, *Collecting Model Trains*, Mark Haber & Co., 1956

—, *The Toy Collector*, Hawthorn Books/Thomas Y. Crowell Co., 1967; Funk & Wagnalls, New York, 1969

Hervé, Gilles and Parry-Crooke, Charlotte (ed.), *Great Toys: Märklin 1895–1914*, Denys Ingram Publishers, London/Editions d'Art Monelle Hayot, Paris/Orell Füssli Verlag, Zurich, 1983

Hollander, Ron, *All Aboard*, Workman Publishing Co., Inc., New York, 1981

Huntingdon, Barnard, *Along Hornby Lines*, Oxford Publishing Co., Oxford, 1976

Joyce, J., *Collectors' Guide to Model Railways*, Model and Allied Publications, Argus Books, Hemel Hempstead, Hertfordshire, 1977

Kampmann, Joachim, *Märklin-Chronik 125 Jahre 1859–1984*, Mikado Verlags-und-Vertriebs-GmbH, 1984

Kimball, Ward, *Toys: Delights from the Past*, Applied Arts Publishers, 1978

King, Constance Eileen, *The Encyclopedia of Toys*, Robert Hale, London, 1978; reprinted New Burlington Books, London, 1985

Kowal, Case, *Toy Trains of Yesteryear*, Model Craftsman Publishing Co., 1972

Krames, Bill and Schroder, Al, *Dad's Trains and Grandad's Too*, Bill Krames, 1958

Lamming, Clive, *Cents Ans de Trains Jouets en France*, La Vie du Rail, Paris, 1981

—, *Les Jouets Anciens*, Editions Atlas, Paris, 1982

Levy, Allen, *A Century of Model Trains*, New Cavendish Books, London, 1974

Matzke, Eric, *Greenberg's Guide to Marx Trains*, Greenberg Publishing Co., Sykesville, Maryland, 1978

McComas, Tom and Tuohy, James, *Lionel: A Collector's Guide and History volume I: Pre-war Gauge O*, T.M. Productions, 1975

—, *Lionel: A Collector's Guide and History volume III: Standard Gauge*, T.M. Productions, 1978

McCrindell, Ron, *Toy Trains*, Salamander Books, London, 1985

McDuffie, Al, Vagner, Richard, Greenberg, Bruce, Clement, Richard, Brophy, John, Zabriskie, George and Collins, Charles, *Greenberg's Guide to Ives Trains 1901–1932*, Greenberg Publishing Co., Sykesville, Maryland, 1984

Minns, J.E., *Model Railway Engines*, Weidenfeld & Nicolson, London, 1969

Murray, Patrick, *Toys*, Studio Vista, London/Dutton Paperbacks, New York, 1968

Pressland, David, *The Art of the Tin Toy*, New Cavendish Books, London, 1976

Randall, P.E., *Recent Locomotives 1947–1970*, Thomas Nelson, Walton-on-Thames, 1970

Reder, Gustav, *Clockwork, Steam and Electric: A History of Model Railways up to 1939*, Ian Allan, Shepperton, Middlesex, 1972

Reher, Uwe, *Eisenbahn Spielzeug*, Verlag Eisenbahn/Hobby Haas, Frankfurt am Main, 1977

Remise, Jac, *L'Argus des Jouets Anciens 1850–1918*, André Balland, Paris, 1978

Remise, Jac and Fondin, Jean, *The Golden Age of Toys*, Edita Lausanne, 1967

Steel, E.A. and Steel, E.H., *The Miniature World of Henry Greenly*, Model and Allied Publications, Argus Books, Hemel Hempstead, Hertfordshire, 1973

Weltens, Arno, *Mechanical Tin Toys in Colour*, Blandford Press, Poole, Dorset/Uitgeverij Kosmos bv, Amsterdam, 1977

Williams, Guy R., *The World of Model Trains*, André Deutsch, London, 1970

REPRODUCTIONS OF MANUFACTURERS' ORIGINAL CATALOGUES

Adburgham, Alison (ed.), *Gamage's Christmas Bazaar 1913*, David & Charles, Newton Abbot, Devon, 1974

Baecker, Carlernst and Hass, Dieter, *Die Anderen Nürnberger*, Hobby Haas Verlag, Frankfurt am Main

    Volume 1: Karl Bub; Georges Carette & Cie; Johann Distler K.G.; Doll & Cie, 1973

Volume 2: J. Falk; Günthermann (S.G.); Gebrüder Fleischmann; Jos Kraus & Co.; Ernst Paul Lehmann, 1973

Volume 3: Johann Andreas Issmayer; Ernst Plank; Georg Levy; Tipp & Co., 1974

Volume 4: Gebrüder Einfalt (Kosmos); Emil Hausmann, Jean Schönner; Conrad Klein; A. Schumann (A.S.), 1975

Volume 5: Karl Arnold; Moses Kohnstam (Moko); Karl Bub; R. & G.N.: Georges Carette; Schreyer & Co. (Schuco), 1976

Volume 6: Ernst Paul Lehmann; Ullmann & Engelmann; Trix, 1981

Baecker, Carlernst, Hass, Dieter and Jeanmaire, Claude, *Technical Toys in the Course of Time*

Volume 1: *Märklin (1859–1902): From the Foundation to the Turn of the Century*, Hobby Haas Verlag, Frankfurt am Main, 1975

Volume 2: *Märklin (1904–1908): In the Emperor's Time, up to 1908*, Hobby Haas, 1976

Volume 3: *Märklin (1891–1915): The Toy Railways from 1891 until 1915*, Verlag Eisenbahn, 1979

Volume 4: *Märklin (1909–1912): New Ways to Success up to 1912*, Hobby Haas, 1978

Volume 5: Karl Arnold; Moses Kohnstam (Moko); Karl Bub; R. & G.N.; Georges Carette; Schreyer & Co. (Schuco), 1976

Volume 6: *Märklin (1919–1921): New Horizons up to 1921*, Hobby Haas, 1980

Volume 7: *Märklin (1923–1927): The New Sales Catalogues*, Hobby Haas, 1981

Volume 8: to be published

Volume 9: *Märklin (1928–1929): The Golden Twenties*, Hobby Haas, 1983

Volume 10: *Märklin (1902–1978): The Small Gauges OO/HO*, Verlag Eisenbahn, 1979

Baecker, Carlernst and Jeanmaire, Claude, *Technical Toys in the Course of Time Volume 11: Märklin: (1930–1931) Focus on the Reichsbahn*, Hobby Haas Verlag, Frankfurt am Main, 1984

Blenken, Jan, Richter, Rolf and Rossig, Reinhard, *Ernst Plank (1903)*, Weinheimer Auktionshaus, 1973

Gorman, F.R., *Hornby Book of Trains (1927–1932)*, Oxford Publishing Co., Oxford, 1973

Jeanmaire, Claude, *Die Weiten Spuren (Märklin 1891–1968)*, Verlag Eisenbahn, 1969

—, *Bing: Die Modellbahnen Unserer Grossväter (Bing 1882–1933) (Grandad's Model Railways)*, Verlag Eisenbahn, 1972

—, *Gebrüder Bing: Die Grossen Nürnberger (1902–1904)*, Verlag Eisenbahn, 1974

Jeanmaire, Claude, *Toys of Nuremberg, Jean Schönner's Toy Railways and Ships*, Verlag Eisenbahn, 1977

Levy, Allen, *Bassett-Lowke Railways (1902–1963)*, Basset-Lowke (Railways) Ltd, Northampton, 1968

—, *The Great Toys of Georges Carette (1905, 1911, 1914)*, New Cavendish Books, London, 1975

Nicholls, Mike and Smith, Paul, *The Life Story of Meccano by Frank Hornby: Meccano Magazine 1932–3*, New Cavendish Books, London, 1976

Parry-Crooke, Charlotte (ed.), *Toys · Dolls · Games: Paris 1903–1914*, Denys Ingram Publishers, London/Hastings House Publishers Inc., New York, 1981

—, *Mr Gamage's Great Toy Bazaar (1902 · 1906)*, Denys Ingram Publishers, London/Hastings House Publishers Inc., New York, 1982

Randall, Peter, *Main Line Ending, Meccano Magazine Digest, 1940–1963*, The Cranbourn Press

—, *The Story of Gauge O Hornby Trains: Articles from the Meccano Magazine (1922–1929)*, The Cranbourn Press, 1974

Truin, Ronald, *Meccano Magazine, Hornby Digest: 1924–1939*, The Cranbourn Press,

ACKNOWLEDGEMENTS

I should like to thank all the people who have helped with this book by offering comments, giving photographs and loaning trains from their collections: Colin Baddiel, Bill Becker, David Burt, Dave Cole, Peter and Joan Dunk, Burt Ehrlich, William "Fin" Finlason, Betty Hale, Dana Hawkes of Sotheby's, New York, Andrew Hilton of Phillips, London, Hilary Kay of Sotheby's, London, Paul Klein-Schiphorst, Ted Leech, Allen Levy and the London Toy and Model Museum, Anthony Manthos, Anna Marrett of Phillips, London, Tim Matthews of Christies, South Kensington, London, Tim Morris, Nigel Mynheer of Phillips, London, Nicolas Oddy, David Pressland, Kerry Taylor of Sotheby's London, Stuart Waldman and Steve Willats.

INDEX

Page numbers in *italics* refer to captions